W9-BVF-873

The Ethical Decision-Making Manual for Helping Professionals

Sarah O. Steinman, PhD

Nan Franks Richardson, MA, CCDC III

Tim McEnroe

Brooks/Cole Publishing Company

I(T)P® An International Thomson Publishing Company

Pacific Grove • Albany • Belmont • Bonn • Boston • Cincinnati • Detroit • Johannesburg • London
Madrid • Melbourne • Mexico City • New York • Paris • Singapore • Tokyo • Toronto • Washington

Sponsoring Editor: *Eileen Murphy*
Editorial Assistant: *Susan Carlson*
Marketing Team: *Jean Thompson,*
  Romy Taormina, and Deanne Brown
Production Service and Design: *Scratchgravel*
  Publishing Services

Production Coordinator: *Mary Vezilich*
Manuscript Editor: *Betty Berenson*
Cover Design: *William Barrett*
Printing and Binding: *Patterson Printing*

For more information, contact:

BROOKS/COLE PUBLISHING COMPANY
511 Forest Lodge Road
Pacific Grove, CA 93950
USA

International Thomson Editores
Seneca 53
Col. Polanco
11560 México, D. F., México

International Thomson Publishing Europe
Berkshire House 168-173
High Holborn
London WC1V 7AA
England

International Thomson Publishing Japan
Hirakawacho Kyowa Building, 3F
2-2-1 Hirakawacho
Chiyoda-ku, Tokyo 102
Japan

Thomas Nelson Australia
102 Dodds Street
South Melbourne, 3205
Victoria, Australia

International Thomson Publishing Asia
221 Henderson Road
#05-10 Henderson Building
Singapore 0315

Nelson Canada
1120 Birchmount Road
Scarborough, Ontario
Canada M1K 5G4

International Thomson Publishing GmbH
Königswinterer Strasse 418
53227 Bonn
Germany

Printed in the United States of America

10   9   8   7   6   5   4   3   2   1

Library of Congress Cataloging-in-Publication Data
Steinman, Sarah O., [date]–
    The ethical decision-making manual for helping professionals /
Sarah O. Steinman, Nan Franks Richardson, Tim McEnroe.
        p.   cm.
    Includes index.
    ISBN 0-534-34939-0 (alk. paper)
    1. Counselors—Professional ethics.   2. Social service—Moral and
ethical aspects.   3. Decision-making (Ethics)—Problems, exercises,
etc.   I. Richardson, Nan Franks.   II. McEnroe, Tim, [date]–   .
III. Title.
BF637.C6S764   1998
174'.9362—dc21   97-30372
                                                                 CIP

CONTENTS

PART II
Ethical Principles for Helping Professionals

CHAPTER 4
Personal Responsibilities

CHAPTER 5
Client Welfare and Client Relationships

CHAPTER 12

Suggested Resolutions of Ethical Dilemmas   91

Index   127

ABOUT THE AUTHORS

Sarah O. Steinman, now in private practice, was assistant professor in the Department of Allied Health, Human Services and Social Work at Northern Kentucky University, Highland Heights, where she taught classes on ethics for helping professionals for nearly 5 years. A licensed psychologist, she earned her MA and PhD in clinical psychology at the University of Cincinnati. Besides her academic work, Dr. Steinman has practical experience in group, couples, and individual therapy.

Nan Franks Richardson is active as a counselor and trainer and serves as executive director of the Alcoholism Council of Cincinnati, NCADD. She holds a BA in philosophy and an MA in rehabilitation counseling, is certified as a chemical dependency counselor, and is a licensed professional counselor. Especially well known for her training skills, Ms. Richardson conducts frequent workshops on ethics for helping professionals as well as workshops on dependency and codependency issues.

Tim McEnroe is a professional writer and former newspaper columnist. He is the co-author, with Ms. Richardson, of a workbook on ethics for chemical dependency counselors.

PREFACE

This manual was designed to be used by college instructors at undergraduate and graduate levels and by workshop instructors who teach the subject of ethics to students preparing to work in one of the helping professions. As a manual, its purpose is more limited than that of college-level texts on the subject—it is an application-oriented effort to guide current and future helping professionals to develop a thinking process that will help them avoid ethical problems in their work and lead them to satisfactory resolutions of those they cannot avoid.

We present and discuss the ethical codes of eight major professional organizations. But before we get to the specific ethical standards, we describe and discuss ways to avoid what we believe are the most common reasons for ethical violations—what we refer to as ethical traps.

The reader will note that the one common theme in these traps is recognition of personal responsibility. Professional ethical problems are not abstractions—they involve real people in real situations, and one of these real people is the helping professional. This means that staying out of these traps requires a strong sense of ethical self-awareness, a subject that most of us spend little time examining. But, as we show in this book, our own ethical standards are at least as likely as those of our clients to cause ethical problems.

Since ethical self-awareness is such an important part of ethical decision making, we have included a self-assessment evaluation tool to help readers raise the level of their own self-awareness regarding these issues and to stimulate thinking and discussion.

Other features of this book include:

- Our suggestions for a step-by-step decision-making process for examining and resolving any professional ethical dilemma
- Almost 50 real-life ethical dilemmas for discussion and resolution
- Worksheet forms based on our decision-making process to accustom readers to looking at ethical dilemmas in a systematic way
- A discussion of how we would resolve each dilemma using the decision-making process outlined in the book

We also include a special section on ethics for supervisors. Although this may seem unusual for what is essentially a teaching tool, in our experience people in the helping professions often are given supervisory responsibilities early and can use this kind of guidance. Perhaps more important, those who are entering the profession have a right to know what ethical standards they should hold their supervisors to. These are spelled out here.

The ethical principles outlined and discussed in this book are compiled from the standards published for their members by the

American Association for Marriage and Family Therapy

American Counseling Association

American Psychological Association

Association of Guidance and School Counselors

National Association of Alcohol and Drug Abuse Counselors

National Association of Social Workers

National Board for Certified Counselors

National Organization for Human Service Education

Although all these standards are similar in intent, some differ in their precise wording. We have remained faithful to the intent as we prepared this material.

Additionally, some codes address certain areas of ethical responsibility that others do not. Since this manual is intended for the use and guidance of all helping professionals, we have chosen to be inclusive and present all ethical principles addressed by any of the standards we have examined and used. Besides understanding the principles as they appear here, practitioners will want to be familiar with the specifics of the standards for their own field.

In our experience as teachers, trainers, and supervisors, students and less experienced professionals believe they won't really have many ethical problems to face, and those they might face will have commonsense, objective solutions apparent to anyone with a pure heart and clear mind, especially themselves.

But in fact, professional care-givers live their working lives in a uniquely intimate and confidential relationship with their clients. This alone means that few will escape serious ethical challenges in their work, and the longer professionals are in the field, the more likely they are to face such challenges. Because it is almost inevitable that a helping professional's ethics will be challenged at some point in his or her career, it makes sense to learn how to resolve ethical dilemmas systematically and satisfactorily before they come up.

This book was reviewed by university-level faculty at three different stages as it developed: Lloyd V. Dempster, Texas A&M University–Kingsville; Jackie Gerstein, College of Santa Fe; Ken Johnson, Amber University; Ronn Johnson, University of San Diego; Lenore Parker, California State University–Fullerton; Ann D. Puryear, Southeast Missouri State University; Daniel L. Segal, University of Colorado at Colorado Springs; Judith R. Slater, Kennesaw State University; and Sharon Wilson, Lorain County Community College. We are grateful for their many insightful comments, which helped shape the book into what it is today.

We are always interested in further comments on this complicated subject and on the book itself and encourage both instructors and students to send us their reactions and suggestions.

Sarah O. Steinman
Nan Franks Richardson
Tim McEnroe

INTRODUCTION

In classroom and workshop sessions, many students and helping professionals early in their careers enjoy few things more than debating the resolution of ethical dilemmas brought to them for discussion. But after a number of years of listening to these discussions as teachers and trainers of helping professionals as well as working in this field ourselves, it has become apparent that students are confused about the most likely source of the ethical dilemmas they will face.

That is, students who are relatively unfamiliar with the subject—and who have not closely examined ethical dilemmas they have faced in their personal lives—believe that professional ethical dilemmas are mostly client-driven. Their common supposition is that should they face ethical challenges as helping professionals, those they face will be caused by their clients alone and that it will be their job to sort things out and supply answers that are clearly "right" under the circumstances.

One thing that makes this kind of thinking misleading is the relative complexity of the ethical codes and their relationship in some cases to the law. But what also makes this kind of thinking misleading is the fact that all professional ethical dilemmas include the professional as an active participant—not just as a "judge"—and many, if not most, are actually caused by the helping professional, often in the course of trying to do the right thing for his or her clients.

This manual will help students understand the ethical codes of a number of organizations of helping professionals. But, more important, it will help them understand the role that they and their own values and belief systems will play in both the creation and resolution of ethical challenges in their professional lives.

Is this subject really important? The answer is yes, and the more experience a helping professional gains in her or his chosen field, the more common ethical challenges become. An October 1995 survey of human services students, faculty, and practitioners in a state college system underscores this point dramatically. It shows that although about half of the students had "ever faced a serious ethical dilemma" in connection with their role as students, all but one of the faculty member respondents and 70% of the practitioner respondents said they had faced such a dilemma at one point or another in their professional careers. In this connection, it's interesting to note that college courses, workshops, and ethical codes were all ranked as among the most influential factors in resolving these dilemmas by all three categories of respondents.

Recognition of helping professionals' own responsibilities for ethical dilemmas and using this recognition to learn how to avoid ethical traps and resolve those that can't be avoided are what this book is all about.

PART I

Ethics and You

CHAPTER 1

The Ethical Traps

Without the aid of trained emotions the intellect is powerless against the animal organism. I had sooner play cards against a man who was quite skeptical about ethics, but bred to believe that "a gentleman does not cheat," than against an irreproachable moral philosopher who had been brought up among sharpers.

C. S. Lewis, "The Abolition of Man"

Ethical Trap 1: The "Commonsense, Objectivity" Trap

Ethical Trap 1 is a belief that "commonsense, objective solutions" to professional ethical dilemmas are always easy to come by because helping professionals are basically ethical people who will use this important personal characteristic as a satisfactory guide when they face any ethical dilemma.

There are two reasons why this is a trap:

- One is the fact that some decisions that appear to be based on ethical considerations must in fact be guided by the law. This is especially true for decisions involving confidentiality and client privacy rights and the treatment of minors, but this is true in other situations as well. And even some of the ethical standards that are not affected by law make little sense unless the reason for them is understood.
- The other, more important, reason is the fact that objectivity—perhaps especially in ethical matters—is an ideal that in real-life situations is very difficult to achieve. Any ethical dilemma helping professionals face on the job will involve them personally as a participant; if it didn't, it wouldn't be theirs to face. And since even professional caregivers are first human beings, they all bring their own very human instincts to any ethical decision they confront, both personal and professional.

This means that many of the ethical dilemmas any practitioner will face professionally—and probably personally as well—will likely be elevated to the condition of "serious" by what she or he brings to the situation. As a result, the answer to the problem may well be and probably is in the ethical code of the individuals' profession, but the difficulty they will have in resolving it satisfactorily—and perhaps the reason it came up in the first place—will likely be in themselves.

A large part of what individuals bring to their profession involves their view of their own experiences—the unique view they have of how the world works in relation to them and their place in it and how well it's working to meet their personal needs. This unique view and the way in which it has been formed often stands in the way of "commonsense, objective" solutions to ethical problems and presents a very real trap in the path of sound professional ethical decisions.

We are all hostages to our own experiences and what we learn from them. And much of what we learn from each experience involves what we think we or others did to influence the way in which a situation turned out. From this learning, we make generalizations that we then apply to the next situation that seems similar. The problem is that we often learn the wrong things from our experiences and thus make and apply the wrong generalizations. When this happens, we can fall into an ethical trap that's difficult to climb out of.

The 19th-century essayist Charles Lamb illustrates this point in a story he wrote about how prehistoric humans learned to cook pork.

In his story, partly domesticated pigs rooting for food ran in and out of the wooden huts in a village. At one point, lightning struck a hut, which then caught fire, trapping a pig in it. The pig was killed by the fire and, in effect, roasted.

One of the more adventurous—and presumably hungry—villagers cut off a piece of the roasted pig and ate it. It was far tastier than anything he had previously eaten. That villager told the others, and they had a feast.

From then on, according to Lamb, whenever the villagers wanted to have a feast, they set someone's hut on fire and threw a pig into it.

Presumably someone later made the more appropriate generalization that a pig could be roasted without burning down a hut, but the point is that what these villagers learned from their experience was that they had to burn down someone's home to get a tasty meal.

As was true for those prehistoric villagers, even the wrong things we learn from our own experiences form our sense of reality. As professionals, we bring our own sense of reality—with all its flaws—to our ethical decision making. This can lead to inappropriate resolutions that can be injurious to ourselves and to our clients.

The other way in which a personal worldview sometimes inappropriately shapes and limits objectivity is through an individual's sense of his or her own personal needs and how well they are being met.

The pressure to meet what are seen as unmet or inadequately met needs often becomes the most important force driving behavior in an individual's personal and professional lives and sometimes blurs the distinction between the two. In our desire to find security, esteem, or intimacy, or to fill some other basic need in our lives, we sometimes sacrifice objectivity and common sense in situations in which they must be applied to find appropriate and satisfactory solutions, especially in our professional lives.

One or both of these reality distorters and objectivity barriers—learning inappropriate lessons from our experiences and putting our own human needs ahead of our professional responsibilities—can create some very real ethical traps. Consider, for example, the following problems that can arise:

- The "reality" for some male counselors is that women are less competent than men and for some whites it is that African Americans are less competent than whites. Those who believe these differences are "real" can justify any form of discrimination against women or African Americans, even though all forms of discrimination are specifically prohibited by all ethical codes.
- The "reality" for some professionals is that the boundaries between personal and professional lives are either nonexistent or unimportant. They may thus believe that what others might see as inappropriate boundary violations—touching clients, unnecessar-

ily asking intimate questions, hugging or kissing clients, telling off-color jokes, or even having sexual relationships with clients—are perfectly justifiable acts, despite counter-indicating professional ethical requirements.

- The "reality" for some helping professionals is that they are paid far less than they should be for their work, given its importance to society and their clients. Those who believe this can justify anything that will increase their income, including conduct that is forbidden by ethical codes.
- The "reality" for some professional care-givers is that they receive far too little recognition and appreciation for what they do. Those who believe this may justify talking about and even inflating their professional accomplishments even when doing so might violate client privacy rights and the ethical codes designed to protect clients.

Since this personal sense of reality—with all its distortions—for most of us is a far more powerful and influential force guiding the way in which we behave than any professional ethical code, it is also far more likely than it should be to influence the way in which we respond to ethical challenges.

This is the reason why in our experience the two most frequently violated ethical codes are also the two that are most explicit in every ethical code for counselors since Hippocrates—and should be the most obvious: the requirements that professional care-givers not reveal private information about their clients and refrain from having sexual relationships with them. Those who violate these codes are not necessarily ignorant of them. They have consciously or unconsciously overridden them because of their sense of their own reality or personal needs and have thus fallen into Ethical Trap 1.

There are two important lessons that should be learned from this discussion:

1. The observance of professional codes of ethics requires of each practitioner something more fundamental than learning the specifics of the ethical codes outlined and discussed in this book. It also requires that you know yourself and your own "reality" and personal needs well enough to recognize the circumstances under which you are most likely to fall into an ethical trap.

This, in turn, requires of helping professionals an honest self-examination —with or without professional help—as the first step toward learning how to successfully resolve ethical problems.

In our experience, failure on the part of helping professionals to take this first step is the largest single reason for individual ethical problems. A self-assessment method to help determine possible trouble spots is included in Chapter 2 of this book.

2. Because real objectivity is so difficult to achieve, those who face ethical challenges should never attempt to resolve them entirely on their own. Consultation with supervisors and experienced and respected peers to clarify real issues and remove personal biases when ethical problems arise should always be undertaken as a good defense against Ethical Trap 1.

Ethical Trap 2: The "Values" Trap

Ethical Trap 2, the second major reason for individual ethical problems, is a confusion on the part of many helping professionals about what professional ethical codes are and what they are not. Personal values, moral standards, and religious convictions are important influences for most people on the way in which they act, but they are not professional ethical codes. And when practitioners substitute what these influences teach them for the explicit provisions of their professional ethical codes (often a great temptation), they can fall into Ethical Trap 2.

These definitions will be helpful:

- Professional ethical codes are generally accepted systems of conduct designed to guide the on-the-job behavior of individuals in a profession in their working relationships with their clients, their employers, their communities, and their peers. All organizations of helping professionals we know of have such ethical codes, which are sometimes referred to as "standards." Most disciplines require that practitioners formally agree to abide by the ethical code of their profession when they receive their credentials or licenses.

- Personal values are priority systems all individuals have—whether they acknowledge it or not—and use to determine what is more important and what is less important to them. These personal value systems are frequently used as a guide in making major decisions. For example, a choice to work overtime rather than spend more time with one's family is a personal value-driven decision (the extra money has a higher priority than the extra time with the family). Some people are said to "have no values," but the fact is that everyone has values, and individuals seen as having none actually have values that differ from our own or from what we see as the norm.

- Moral standards are codes of personal behavior used primarily as a guide to conduct in everyday lives, especially in social relationships with others. Unlike personal values, which rate priorities, moral standards are generally absolute and positive (I will be honest, I will be faithful to my sexual partner, and so on), but are frequently put into use as personal prohibitions (I will not cheat at cards, I will not cheat on my partner, etc.). Sometimes these moral codes are based on religious convictions (see below). Along with personal values, we all have a moral code with which we guide our behavior, though we may not label it as such. Those who are seen as "immoral" (that is, without morals) actually have moral standards with which others disagree.

- Religious beliefs for people who hold them often guide both the value systems and the moral standards they set for themselves and a sense of what is "right" and "wrong" behavior in others. Those who use religious convictions to guide their own behavior and their judgments about that of others see these convictions as having special force because in their view these convictions have been handed down by a higher spiritual power and thus override temporal authority. A decision to stay in an unfulfilling marriage because doing so "is the right thing to do" because of a past commitment is a moral standard applied by an individual to him- or herself. Doing so because divorce is sinful for everyone is a judgment based on a religious conviction.

As you think through these definitions and the ways in which you apply them to your personal life, you'll probably see how easy and tempting it is to apply them automatically to the ethical aspects of your professional life as well. People who go into helping professions are generally individuals who are strongly motivated by a desire to help others solve their problems and are firm in their belief that they themselves have accurate moral compasses that will unerringly lead them to sound ethical decisions.

But the fact still remains that sometimes what is required of helping professionals by their professional ethical codes may seem to conflict with their own personal values, moral standards, or religious convictions and thus set up ethical traps.

For example, a counselor or therapist who holds a strong religious conviction that homosexuality is fundamentally wrong can easily justify either refusing to counsel homosexuals or making a client's sexual orientation the major therapeutic issue, despite the prohibition in all ethical codes against discrimination on the basis of sexual preference.

As another example, those who have a strong bias against divorce or one in favor of keeping families with children together regardless of other considerations can easily justify urging a mother in an abusive relationship to stay with her children's father despite the ethical requirement that the client's interests should be paramount.

While you're studying and thinking through the ethical standards of your discipline, you'll no doubt find other examples of possible conflicts, each of which is an ethical trap that's easy to fall into. The important thing to remember is that in your professional life when professional codes conflict with your own beliefs—no matter how sound these beliefs may be or how important you think they are to yourself and others—you must use the professional codes as the basis of your decision making.

One last point here: In recent years an increasing number of professional activities have come to be regulated by the law, and such legal regulations sometimes at least appear to be violations of both professional ethical requirements and personal and religious moral codes. When this happens, professionals need to think through their responses carefully—and always in consultation with supervisors and with attorneys who are familiar with such issues. In general, when such conflicts appear, helping professionals should obey the law. Those who don't can fall into another kind of trap—a legal trap—and take their organizations in with them. In some cases, though, it may be important to society, to the profession, or to an individual client that the law be challenged. But this should be done only after consultation and a careful evaluation of the consequences of such a challenge.

Ethical Trap 3: The "Circumstantiality" Trap

The third ethical trap is a belief that there are no "right" or "wrong" answers to any ethical questions because the circumstances under which they occurred (rather than the behavior itself) must be taken into consideration in making the decision. However, while it is true that some behavior may or may not be an ethical violation depending on circumstances, this is not always the case; behavior is often either right or wrong according to professional ethical standards regardless of the circumstances under which it occurred.

Many ethical dilemmas are complicated and difficult to resolve satisfactorily. But what frequently makes them appear more complicated and difficult than they should be is excessive concern about circumstances. In some cases this makes sense. In other cases it does not.

Professional ethical standards are guides to acceptable and unacceptable behavior on the part of members of a particular profession. The standards have been carefully developed over a period of time to protect the interests of the profession, the individuals served by the profession, the public, and the professionals themselves. The standards are, in this sense, much like traffic laws designed to protect drivers and those who might be injured by drivers. These laws say you must stop at red lights, obey speed limits, signal before you make a turn, and so on. They are not either suggestions or options; they say what drivers must do. If you violate one of them and are caught, you get a ticket.

In many cases, neither the violation of these laws nor the consequences of doing so can be mitigated by circumstances. There are, for example, no circumstances under which it is legally acceptable for someone who is impaired by drugs to drive a car.

But every driver knows that there are circumstances under which violating one of these laws may be prudent or in some cases even necessary. For example:

Many drivers faced with a red light at an intersection at 3 A.M. when there is no other traffic will look around to be sure it is safe to run the light and then do so.

A prospective father driving a partner who is about to give birth to the hospital may believe it necessary to ignore speed limits in order to get help in time.

In both cases, while the driver may deserve a ticket for the violation, a police officer or judge could very well determine that the circumstances of the violation were such that no punishment should be given.

But in these cases, it is the consequence of the violation that would be circumstantially determined and not the violations themselves, since violations did occur.

Below are three ethical examples for thought and discussion:

1. Ethical codes prohibit counselors and other helping professionals from accepting gifts from clients. Say that you are a mental health counselor of a client who is a graphic artist. This client has designed and produced a calendar that features her work. At the end of your regular counseling session, she gives you a copy. What do you do?
2. Ethical codes require that the fact that an individual is being treated for a mental illness not be revealed to anyone without the client's permission. Say that you are on duty in a group home for persons with various mental illnesses. One of the residents has not taken his medications, destabilizes, and becomes violent to the point at which you need to call the police in order to protect him, the other residents, and, perhaps, members of the public from possible harm. What do you tell the police about this individual's condition when they arrive?
3. Ethical codes prohibit helping professionals from having sexual relationships with their clients. Say that you are a drug abuse counselor and you believe that your client is no longer using drugs and that her poor self-esteem would be enhanced by a fulfilling sexual relationship with you, and she agrees with this assessment. Is it okay to have a sexual relationship with her?

As is probably obvious in thinking about these three dilemmas, they represent the two ends and the middle of the scale in which the circumstances should be taken into consideration.

1. The question of whether it is ethically correct to accept a gift from a client almost always requires a resolution based on circumstances. The intrinsic value of the gift, when in the course of the professional relationship it is offered, its real meaning in a psychological sense, and other circumstances all need to be considered in determining whether acceptance is ethical. Clearly accepting monetary gifts beyond fees is unethical, as would be accepting an object of significant intrinsic value. On the other hand, acceptance of the calendar mentioned in the example would be ethically permissible because of the circumstances, and rejection of it might even cause some therapeutic harm. The calendar could even be hung in a public space to share the gift with others. If, however, the client were a painter whose work commanded high prices and the gift was one of her paintings, the answer would be different because the circumstances would be different.
2. Protection of a client's right to privacy is one of the most important of the ethical codes for every helping profession. Knowledge of the fact that an individual is receiv-

ing some sort of therapeutic or even financial assistance could lead to harm for the client in one form or another, and it is the ethical responsibility of helping professionals to protect their clients from this potential harm. In the circumstances contained in the example, however, there are good reasons why in many ethical codes this kind of situation is specifically mentioned as an exception to confidentiality rules. These reasons include protecting the client himself from harm, the interests of the other residents, the possible interests of members of the general public, and the interests of the police officers who are being called in to help. Protecting all of these interests has greater weight under these circumstances than does protecting the privacy rights of this particular client. You should give the police whatever information they need to bring the situation under control. The circumstances suggest that you should take this step regardless of what a strict interpretation of the code might say, and these circumstances should then be used to determine the consequences, if any.

3. There are no circumstances under which it is ethically correct to have sexual relations with a client, nor are there any circumstances that could mitigate the consequences for having done so.

Perhaps as a reaction to what many believe was excessive rigidity in the past in making decisions about what is "right" and "wrong" behavior, there is a tendency in contemporary life to refrain from making any such judgments about any behavior without a complete understanding of the circumstances under which it occurred. It is certainly useful in therapeutic settings to be "nonjudgmental" about a client's activities in order to help the client address in a nonadversarial way her or his internal needs to engage in those activites. And there is nothing wrong about refraining from judging one's own and others' behavior without first understanding and weighing all the circumstances leading to the behavior. But holding ourselves to the ethical standards of our own profession is not an option that is determined by surrounding circumstances. Doing so is right, not doing so is wrong, and believing otherwise is an ethical trap.

It can also be a legal trap. While ethical standards do not themselves have the force of law in civil and criminal courts, their violation can often be a determining factor in a lawsuit involving charges of malpractice. That is, if the behavior of a helping professional leads to a lawsuit by a client or someone affected by a client's behavior against a care-giver or his or her agency, the fact that the behavior was specifically prohibited by the ethical standards of the individual's profession could have a substantial impact on the outcome of the lawsuit.

Ethical Trap 4: The "Who Will Benefit" Trap

The fourth ethical trap helping professionals can easily fall into results from confusion about who will benefit from a specific ethical decision.

Though it's not often expressed or even recognized, one thing that frequently turns a situation into an ethical dilemma that is difficult to resolve is the fact that a decision may result in both a "winner" and a "loser." That is, resolving an ethical dilemma often means taking sides from among two or more conflicting interests, and that makes many of us uncomfortable.

Since one of the most frequently quoted axioms in the helping professions is "put the client's interest first," it would appear that this is the answer to the "who will benefit" question. Though this is most often the case, it's sometimes not that easy.

One reason is that it's the long-term rather than short-term interests of a client that need to be put first in ethical considerations. Doing so sometimes requires a different decision than the one that would be dictated by applying only short-term considerations. That is, say, for example, that you determine that a client of yours is about to commit a burglary, the details of which he has revealed to you in the course of counseling. Putting the short-term interests of the client first suggests that you maintain confidentiality and not interfere with your client's potential behavior. But since it is at least likely that your client will be caught and punished, his long-term interests might better be protected by informing him that you are required to report this potential act to the authorities.

Additionally, there are sometimes potential winners and losers involved in ethical decisions who have a higher claim as potential beneficiaries than that of your client. We call this ranking of potential beneficiaries of ethical decisions when interests are in conflict the "ethical hierarchy." We suggest it be used as a guide to determine whose interests should come first in such cases. While this hierarchy is not spelled out specifically in any ethical code, it is our view that it should be used except in those situations in which the law or state or federal regulations require something different.

The Ethical Hierarchy

The Professional as Professional

Helping professionals have a responsibility to ensure that they refrain from any behavior that would jeopardize their ability to continue to work in their professional field. Because of their education and training, expertise, specialized knowledge and insights, and—often—official certification by their state or professional organization, they are important assets to all their clients specifically and to society as a whole generally. This means that when professionals have an ethical choice to make, they should ensure that in doing so they do not put themselves in a position that might limit or eliminate their value as professionals to others. Thus, even in a situation of long-term benefit to an individual client, if making a decision that benefits him or her puts the care-giver in a dangerous position professionally, practitioners should put their interests—that is, the interests of their other clients—first.

As an example, consider that hospitalization insurance benefits for those with mental illnesses or who abuse substances are shrinking under managed care. In many cases, clients whose condition was considered severe enough to require hospitalization in recent years are no longer eligible for it. Professionals who deal with clients with these conditions are often tempted to inflate or fabricate diagnoses in an effort to gain for the client the hospital treatment they think the client needs. Though this may be considered humane from the point of view of the professional, it is a dangerous activity for the professional because in many cases doing so is illegal and getting caught could cause revocation of her or his credentials and ability to practice.

As another example, professionals sometimes need to protect their physical and emotional well-being from clients, even those clients who seem to be benefiting from the professional relationship. During the course of their careers, most counselors and therapists will encounter at least one client who threatens them emotionally because of transference or countertransference issues. Often these can be resolved in the course of counseling, but sometimes the counselor's own emotional safety requires withdrawal from the counseling relationship.

Additionally, case managers and counselors of individuals with mental illnesses are sometimes assigned clients who fixate on them in threatening ways. While the possibility of physical abuse is perhaps less common than is emotional abuse, when it exists, helping professionals have every ethical right to put their own interests ahead of those of their client and to take appropriate steps to remove the threat. Such steps can include insisting that the client be assigned to someone else or perhaps even to another agency.

Finally, as indicated earlier, the law in some cases requires counselors to take certain actions that may cause short- and even long-term harm to their clients, such as reporting known or suspected incidents of child abuse. Should you fail to report such incidents in an effort to protect your client, you put yourself at professional and legal risk.

It needs to be emphasized that all this obviously does not mean that professionals may protect themselves and their ability to continue to function as a professional by covering up mistakes, falsifying records, and other such activities. These are, of course, unethical and often illegal activites. The key point is that when making an ethical choice among competing interests in which your own professional interests or personal safety are at stake, you are ethically required to protect yourself emotionally and physically. Besides your personal safety, protecting yourself protects your ability to work in the best interest of *all* your clients as a professional in your field.

Society

The law and regulatory agencies governing helping professionals, especially at the state level, are increasingly reflecting public opinion that our communities have an important stake in the outcome of some decisions—traditionally purely ethical in nature—that may affect others as well as the client. When this is the case it is the interests of the others—society as a whole—that should determine the outcome of these decisions.

For the most part, these laws and regulations involve circumstances under which professionals should—or increasingly must—suspend long-standing client privacy rights, especially in respect to known or suspected criminal activities.

It is argued by some professionals that substituting the law for long-standing ethical principles regarding the confidentiality of what is learned in a therapeutic relationship is fundamentally wrong on at least three counts: (1) doing so will almost surely do irreparable harm to the therapeutic relationship; (2) sending a client to jail violates the age-old principle of putting clients' interests first; (3) such laws, in effect, turn helping professionals into law enforcers (for which they are untrained), which is not their function in society.

It is our belief that putting society's interests ahead of client interests in such cases is entirely appropriate ethically for a number of reasons. For example, if you learn during your professional relationship that a client intends to murder his wife, deciding that his right to privacy is greater than his wife's right to live may protect him in the short run, but that decision in fact may both lead to her murder and put him in prison. In a case like this, there is a legal requirement in most states requiring you to warn both law enforcement authorities and the potential victim. This requirement is also ethically correct because it protects the long-term best interests of the client as well as those of his wife and, by implication, of society.

Another reason is the fact that people who are licensed by their state or credentialing organization to practice their profession (which in one way or another most helping professionals are) have a responsibility to society to see that its rights are preserved and its laws obeyed.

Accepting the license or certification allows us to practice, but it also requires us to do so in a way that is beneficial to society as well as to ourselves and to our individual clients.

It needs to be pointed out that it is society's laws and not its behavioral norms or even shared values that helping professionals are bound to protect. Helping professionals are not thought police. Helping a client understand the way in which his or her behavior isolates him or her from society may be a useful therapeutic goal in counseling, but preserving his or her right to make a choice about adaptation to society's norms is the appropriate ethical outcome. Attempting to remove this choice by imposing a system of "correct" behavior is both unethical and poor therapy.

There is constant tension in our country between the rights of the individual and the rights of society. Where one ends and the other begins is frequently unclear and can shift as public opinion shifts. And as an increasing number of states adopt laws and regulations designed to protect society's interest, tensions between what is ethical and what is legal also develop, often with an equally unclear line of demarcation. These tensions—and lack of clarity—need to be considered when making ethical decisions.

The Individual Client

As indicated above, placing an individual client's interests third rather than first when making ethical choices may seem close to heresy for many helping professionals, but it is not. For while it is true that preserving and enhancing client interests is the basic objective of all who choose this line of work, sometimes there are considerations that make this more complicated than it might seem, and other times when there are actually more important interests than those of the client that require protection.

This does not mean you must become a professional ethicist, lawyer or law enforcement officer as an adjunct to your life as a helping professional, though it may sometimes seem so. It does mean that in order to avoid a fairly deep ethical trap, helping professionals need to be aware that ethical decisions sometimes require tough choices from among competing interests and that it is important to know what those interests are and why they need consideration. Failure to do so may lead to an ethical trap.

CHAPTER 2

Self-Assessment of Professional Ethics

The greater your awareness of your thoughts, feelings, and behavior, the greater your chances to catch ethical dilemmas before they become unethical behaviors. We suggest using this self-assessment tool as a way to increase your understanding of your attitudes about ethical decision making and your current feelings about your role as a helping professional.

Ethical Questionnaire

Read the statements below and circle yes or no depending on how you currently feel about each issue. After completing your answers, refer to the discussion of responses to evaluate your answers and what they reveal about your attitudes. This tool is intended to stimulate your thinking and to help spot potential ethical traps you might fall into. We recommend that you think about your answers and then discuss them with your instructor, a colleague, supervisor, or others.

1. Yes No I have someone with whom I can share almost anything about myself without fear of repercussions.

2. Yes No I believe that I have the ability to be objective and morally accurate when it comes to making difficult ethical decisions.

3. Yes No I am in touch with my own feelings, respectful of them, and will use them to help me understand those of my clients.

4. Yes No I have been eating, drinking, smoking, or sleeping more than I should lately.

5. Yes No I am satisfied with the level of intimacy in my personal life.

6. Yes No Much of the time I feel overwhelmed by what I am expected to do.

7. Yes No I do a good job balancing my time between work and play.

8. Yes No I have adequately dealt with my own personal issues and therefore will be able to keep my personal needs outside of my relationships with clients.

9. Yes   No   I would be willing to seek counseling if I were experiencing personal problems.

10. Yes   No   I am especially attentive to people who find me sexually attractive.

11. Yes   No   I have read a book that has nothing to do with my schoolwork or profession within the last 6 months.

12. Yes   No   I find myself "dressing up" for certain clients.

13. Yes   No   I feel comfortable with the grades I'm getting or the amount of compensation I receive for my professional services.

14. Yes   No   One reason I chose a career as a helping professional is that I feel flattered when people ask me to help them with their problems.

15. Yes   No   I am prepared to respect my client as the ultimate authority on his or her life choices.

16. Yes   No   I consider myself to be a "good person" and therefore will not find myself in violation of any ethical standards.

17. Yes   No   When I have an ethical concern, I won't have any hesitation about seeking advice in resolving it.

18. Yes   No   I think it's important that the people I know understand that I'm helping real people overcome real problems.

19. Yes   No   I am familiar with the ethical codes of my profession.

20. Yes   No   My personal values are the core of who I am as a person and professional and will automatically play a large part in my work.

21. Yes   No   It's okay to consult with colleagues when working with difficult clients, as long as I honor my clients' confidentiality.

22. Yes   No   I expect that the situations I encounter with my clients will often be too complex to fit neatly into the ethical codes of my profession.

23. Yes   No   Even after lots of training, I expect that I won't have all the answers for every client and will feel comfortable making referrals to other competent professionals.

24. Yes   No   In today's society, I believe that there are very few situations that are always "right" or "wrong" because so much depends on the circumstances that surround a specific act or behavior.

25. Yes   No   I think supervision is a valuable tool even for experienced professionals.

26. Yes   No   I expect that most of my clients will have pretty similar stories and problems.

27. Yes   No   Even after my schoolwork and training are completed, there will still be clients I probably won't be able to help.

28. Yes   No   I think that people who seek help from counselors and therapists often exaggerate their distress to get attention.

29. Yes   No   I can identify my own areas of expertise quickly and clearly.

30. Yes   No   Most clients who talk about suicide are really looking for sympathy.

31. Yes   No   I understand that respecting my clients' privacy rights means that I must guard against the most casual mention of specific clients and their problems.

32. Yes   No   What's wrong with people today is that their values aren't what they used to be.

33. Yes   No   My obligation to client confidentiality outweighs my responsibility to my community.

34. Yes   No   Nothing is more important than the personal welfare of my clients.

Discussion of Responses

Questions 1 through 16

As a helping professional, your personal needs and feelings can have an especially strong impact on how you relate to your clients and even on client outcomes. As Abraham Maslow has suggested in his hierarchy of needs, our basic needs for food, shelter, intimacy, belonging, and self-worth must be met in order for us to function in a free and healthy way. Perceptions of deficiencies or problems in these areas will inhibit our ability to be fully professional in our work, possibly clouding judgment in such a way as to cause unethical behavior.

Except for Questions 2, 8, and 16, *yes* answers to odd-numbered questions and *no* answers to even-numbered questions indicate that you are doing a good job of balancing your personal life with your life as a student or practitioner. Questions 2, 8, and 16 relate to the "objectivity" trap discussed in Chapter 1. On the surface, at least, a *yes* answer is appropriate. Be careful, though—your certainty in these areas could lead you into a trap.

No answers to odd-numbered questions and *yes* answers to even-numbered questions indicate that it may be helpful for you to examine your personal needs, satisfaction with the level of support you have in your life, and your relative happiness with yourself as a person. It is important that helping professionals meet their needs in a mature and healthy manner in order to allow them to put their clients' needs above their own in their professional relationships. Although professionals can and should expect some support from their colleagues and organizations, the primary responsibility for self-care—physical, emotional, intellectual, volitional, and spiritual—lies with themselves. It is especially important that helping professionals be open to receiving the same kind of help they would recommend for their clients.

In analyzing your responses to these questions, remember that inappropriate personal relationships with clients and involvement with them in a nonprofessional way are among the most frequent ethical violations by those in helping professions. These violations usually result from a professional's putting his or her personal needs ahead of those of the client.

Questions 17 through 32

Helping professionals need to understand and recognize the limitations to their own personal values, experiences, expertise, and training; be willing to make referrals to other professionals when these limits are exceeded; and accept feedback and suggestions from other professionals.

In general, *yes* answers to odd-numbered questions and *no* answers to even-numbered questions indicate that you have an understanding of the practical limitations you have or will have as a helping professional. As discussed in Chapter 4, ethical codes require a professional to offer treatment or services only within her or his own areas of training, expertise, and understanding and to be willing to seek assistance or referrals when appropriate.

Also, in general, *no* answers to odd-numbered questions and *yes* answers to even-numbered questions indicate that it may be helpful for you to examine the extent to which you might substitute your own values for those of your clients, your understanding of the scope of your knowledge and experience, and your attitudes about accepting help when your understanding is exceeded.

However, watch your answers to Questions 20, 22, 24, and 32, which represent potential traps. Questions 20 and 32 relate to the "values" trap. If you answered *yes* to Question 20 and mean it, you'll be fine, but watch for the trap of pushing your own values at your clients. The appropriate answer to Question 32 is *no*. If you answered *yes*, again watch out for the trap of pushing your own values at your clients. Questions 22 and 24 relate to the "circumstantiality" trap. As indicated above, a *no* answer is appropriate. If you answered *yes*, you might find yourself placing too much focus on the details surrounding your analysis of a situation that is basically either right or wrong ethically.

In analyzing your responses to these questions, remember that offering inappropriate treatment—which sometimes results from projecting personal values onto clients—is among the most frequent ethical violations by those in helping professions.

Questions 33 and 34

These questions relate to possible problems regarding the ethical hierarchy discussed in Chapter 1. A *no* answer is appropriate. A *yes* answer to either question may suggest an inability to recognize situations in which the needs of society outweigh those of your clients. The important thing to remember here is that in some situations, both ethical requirements and the law say you must place other interests ahead of client interests.

CHAPTER 3

The Ethical Decision-Making Process

Ethical dilemmas do not generally come with flags or other signals attached to identify them as such. They are fired point blank during the day-to-day, often minute-by-minute discharge of our professional responsibilities. No one, no matter how experienced or responsible, is immune to the potential of unethical practice. Many ethical violations begin innocently, and some are even an outgrowth of an attempt to offer help. Others may result from ignorance of ethical responsibilities or of falling into any of the traps described in Chapter 1. Oftentimes, the ethical seriousness of a situation slips by us, reemerging perhaps with a stab of concern or guilt during an unrelated conversation with a colleague: "Oh dear, maybe I didn't handle that situation the way I should have. . . ."

It is important that helping professionals have a working familiarity with the ethical requirements of their profession as well as any particular "hot zones" that might exist for them as individuals. Those who have this knowledge can use it as part of an early warning system that alerts them when confronted with a situation that might pose a professional ethical dilemma. Professionals without such knowledge of the ethical codes or of themselves have to rely solely on personal instincts as a signal that things are not as they should be. As indicated earlier, these signals are often wrong. Thus, for such people, all ethical dilemmas will be resolved through the use of personal experience, values, and beliefs, or on the basis of fulfilling personal needs, all of which involve potential ethical traps.

Some ethical dilemmas are more difficult to resolve than they might at first appear. Others initially seem complex but in fact can be resolved simply and easily by applying the relevant principles of an ethical code.

But regardless of the degree of actual difficulty, sound decisions can best be reached by seeing the satisfactory resolution of an ethical dilemma as the result of a step-by-step process that requires consideration of all relevant factors in a systematic way.

The process described in this chapter will be helpful in heading off or resolving ethical problems, but it is most useful if a situation can be identified as a potential problem while still in its "potential" phase. Once an ethical violation has occurred, we also need to examine the consequences and possible rectification of the action already taken rather than the prevention of a bad situation. Prevention is better.

Problem Identification

Deciding what to do about a real or potential ethical problem can't begin until a situation is identified as a possible problem in the first place. This means developing familiarity with professional ethical principles in general (spelled out in Part II) and with the specific principles of your professional discipline. These principles are quite comprehensive, but research has identified the following four problems as the most common sources of professional ethical violations:

- Dual relationships—activities involving professional and client beyond the primary therapeutic or service relationship. These include social and financial relationships as well as sexual ones.
- Breaches of client confidentiality, which often occur unwittingly at the coffee machine or by telling a colleague or co-worker more than he or she needs to know.
- Attempts to provide treatment beyond the scope of an individual's professional competence. This often happens before we realize it, or simply because of requests by a client we want to help.
- Failure to take appropriate steps to prevent suicide attempts.

The point is that no problem can be rectified unless it is first identified as a problem; thus, the decision-making process must begin with recognition that a problem may exist.

Step 1: Identify the Ethical Standard Involved

What is the ethical standard involved?

1. Look at the principles and see what they say. If a code covers the situation, write down what it says. Having done this, find out if there is also a legal requirement involved in the situation. Don't go by your instincts here because there's too much at stake. Consult with a respected colleague or supervisor and recognize that they may want to consult an attorney. If there is a legal issue involved, write that down, too. (Obviously, if there are neither ethical requirements nor laws involved, there isn't really a problem. In this case, you might spend a few minutes thinking about why you thought there might be.)

2. If an examination of the ethical principles still leaves you unclear about whether a violation is involved, consult with a respected peer or supervisor, or call the ethical review board of your profession, explaining the problem and the reasons for your uncertainty.

3. If you find that you are clear about the mandates of your ethical code and any legal requirements that may apply, but you resist or reject the behavior or action they say you should take, it is important to understand why. You may be confronting an unresolved personal issue or an area of clinical expertise in which you need more information. In this connection, it may be helpful to ask yourself if this conflict is a matter of:

- Knowledge (philosophy of treatment or gaps in theoretical knowledge)
- Emotion (involving primarily personal feelings about this client or her or his situation)
- Personal needs (physical, financial, emotional, status/esteem, and so on)

Answers to these questions do not always come easily. You may want to consult with your supervisor, respected peers, or even seek the assistance of a counselor or therapist in order to help mitigate what could be a difficult long-term professional problem.

Step 2: Determine Ethical Trap Possibilities

Is there an ethical trap here?

Think back to the ethical traps discussed earlier. Is one of them involved here? This is an especially important consideration if you are unclear about whether an ethical principle is involved, or if you are convinced one is involved but resist doing what it says you should do.

One signal that an ethical trap may be involved is thinking that this particular situation is especially difficult or, perhaps, even unique. If the circumstances are such that they alone are driving your difficulty, there may be an ethical trap involved.

Step 3: Frame a Preliminary Response

What should an ethical helping professional do?

Look at the notes you have made about what the ethical code (and law) says you should do. Now describe what action you would take based on this analysis.

Make sure your description includes:

- What the code says you should do
- What the law (if any) says you should do
- What circumstances (if any) should influence the response
- The preliminary response

Step 4: Consider the Consequences

What will happen if I take this action?

At first glance, almost any response can look good. But a thoughtful analysis should include an examination of the potential consequences of your response. Neither the short- nor long-term consequences will change what the code or the law says you should do, but one or the other might change the way in which you follow through.

First consider short-term consequences. If you respond in the way your preliminary response indicates, who will be helped? Who will be harmed? One important consideration here is the identification of possible conflicts of interest. Are there conflicts? Between which parties? It is especially important here to identify possible consequences for yourself, since they can powerfully influence your response, perhaps in ways that are ethically inappropriate.

Next consider long-term consequences. Are they different from the short-range consequences? Does your preliminary response (perhaps changed in light of short-term consequences) still hold up in terms of what precedent it might set or long-term behavior it might trigger or encourage? At this point it might be especially important to consider any possible consequences of your preliminary response in terms of your agency or other employer. You should also consider the ethical hierarchy discussed in Chapter 1: Who might be helped or harmed by your preliminary response? Is this appropriate?

In this process, have you uncovered any possible unintended consequences? Will your preliminary response cause something to happen that shouldn't happen to any of the parties involved? One important question here is what a specific response will do to a therapeutic relationship.

Are these consequences ethically defensible; that is, all things considered, is this what the ethical codes seem to have in mind? Would you be able to justify your decision if questioned?

While the answers to these questions about consequences may not change the basic nature of the response, they may change the details. For example, in a situation involving dual relationships, the ethical requirement may be to end the therapeutic relationship because it has become tainted by personal involvement. Should this be the case, the actual response must include consideration of the possible consequences to your client rather than just abrupt termination of the relationship.

Step 5: Prepare Ethical Resolution

Now take your preliminary response and turn it into an ethical resolution.

This will require detailed preparation of a response, plus a listing of potential consequences of taking the action suggested. The proposed resolution should contain:

1. What is the situation, including possible relevant circumstances?
2. What ethical codes or laws are involved?
3. What do these codes or laws suggest I or others do?
4. If I have consulted with colleagues, supervisors, or professional ethics boards at this point, what do they suggest I or others do?
5. What are the consequences of taking this action on the client, on me, on my employer, and on others in the community?
6. In light of these considerations, here is what I propose . . .

Step 6: Get Feedback

Even the most experienced professional needs feedback before resolving an ethical dilemma of any complexity.

Before putting any proposed resolution into action, it is important to discuss it in detail with your supervisor, a respected peer, and, if there are legal issues involved, an attorney. If none of these feedback sources is available or all are inappropriate because of the possibility of conflict of interest, check with the ethics board or review committee of your profession.

Step 7: Take Action

Consider carefully the feedback you've received. Use that feedback to amend your proposed resolution when appropriate. When you're confident about it, take appropriate action.

The flowchart on the following page graphically shows the steps of this ethical decision-making process.

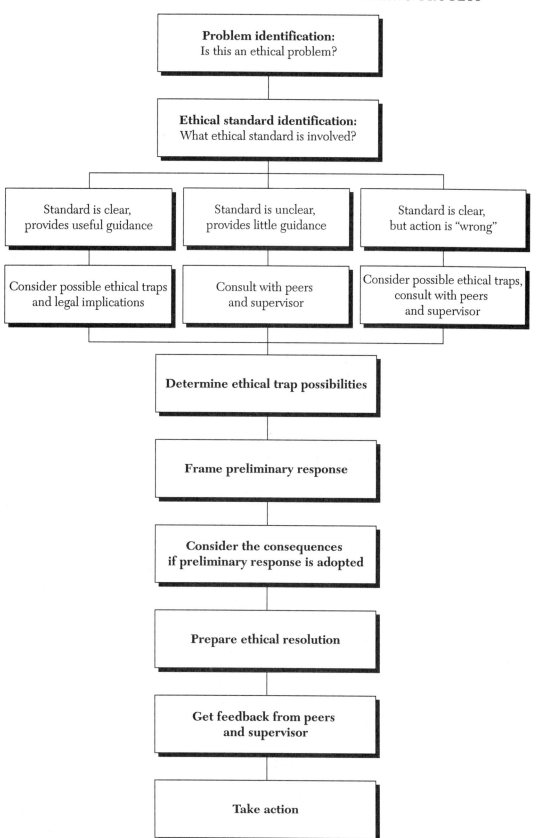

PART II

Ethical Principles for Helping Professionals

The ethical principles outlined and discussed in the next eight chapters are compiled from the standards published for their members by a wide range of organizations of helping professionals. The organizations are named at the beginning of this book. All these standards are similar in intent, though some differ in their precise wording. We have remained faithful to the intent as we prepared the material below. Some specific disciplines within the helping professions address certain areas of ethical responsibility that others do not. Since this manual is intended for the use and guidance of all helping professionals, we have chosen to be inclusive and present all ethical principles addressed by any of the standards we have examined and used. Besides understanding the principles as they appear here, readers will want to be familiar with the specifics of the standards for their own specialty.

As you will note, in each of these chapters we first list the basic ethical standards, follow with a discussion of the behavior required by each, and then suggest some dilemmas that may arise in connection with the requirements. The dilemmas may be thought through and resolved using the decision-making process in Chapter 3. A worksheet based on the steps in the decision-making process is included after each set of dilemmas. The way in which we would resolve each of them is the subject of the last chapter.

CHAPTER 4

Personal Responsibilities

The Ethical Standards

Though helping professionals are like everyone else in most respects, in some important ways they are different. The differences occur because of the helping professional's unique role in society as a trained and frequently licensed resource for individuals in need. These differences include the responsibility to:

- Maintain high standards of personal conduct, recognizing that while helping professionals have the same rights as other individuals in terms of personal behavior, they should not conduct themselves privately in a way that might jeopardize their ability to function professionally.
- Maintain and improve their own professional competence, refrain from practicing in specialties for which they are not specifically trained or professionally experienced, and work to stop unqualified or unauthorized practice in their specialties.
- Actively work to remain free of professional impairment.
- Refrain from discriminating against clients or prospective clients on racial, religious, gender, sexual orientation, economic, or other grounds.
- Develop cultural competence to ensure appropriate services to a diverse population.
- Set fees that recognize both the relative ability of clients to pay them and the helping professional's right to reasonable compensation for his or her services.
- Foster enhanced recognition and understanding in their communities and society as a whole of the impact of special problems and opportunities in their own field.
- Maintain good working relationships with colleagues.
- Advance the standards and interests of their profession.
- Honor commitments to employers and adhere to work rules and codes of practice of the helping professional's organization.

Personal Conduct

Helping professionals should strive to live their personal lives according to ethical principles that are in harmony with those that govern their professional lives and are congruent with behavior sought for and by their clients.

The impact of personal behavior on the effectiveness of the helping professional can be substantial. This fact must be recognized and personal behavior continuously monitored and modified when necessary.

Helping professionals hold a unique public trust because of their training, certification, commitment to their work, and the benefit to society of their profession. Along with their training, one of the major factors determining helping professionals' success is their "personhood"—who they are as individuals. This means that helping professionals have a special responsibility to conduct their lives—both personal and professional—with the highest standards of integrity.

Much research, in fact, identifies a counselor's personal characteristics as having a greater influence on client outcomes than her or his years of professional training or professional credentials. The most important characteristics consistently identified in this research include a capacity for empathy, the ability to respect clients as individuals, the ability to be confrontive when appropriate, and personal authenticity—the standards we set for ourselves and our ability to live, personally and professionally, according to those standards.

Helping professionals are not expected to be perfect and beyond personal problems of their own. And actually, it is often the ways in which they recognize and cope with these problems that make them most effective in their work. There is much wisdom and sensitivity to be gained from the successful resolution of personal struggles that can then be used to help others. Some believe that those who have themselves carried a burden and eventually rid themselves of it are in the best position to help others rid themselves of similar problems.

At the same time, it should be recognized that helping professionals in general—and those engaged in providing therapy and counseling in particular—live in fishbowls through which it is often next to impossible to see a difference between personal and professional conduct.

One obvious example is that of substance abuse counselors. In terms of strict adherence to the ethical standards of that specialty, substance abuse counselors who choose to use alcohol and other drugs when they're not working are free to do so. Abuse of drugs by such counselors, however, presents some very real ethical and therapeutic issues, and even public use in some communities can raise questions.

Furthermore, since we all tend to judge others by our own experiences, abuse of alcohol and other drugs by helping professionals can interfere with their ability to assess abuse and addiction in their clients. Additionally, their need to justify their own abuse is likely to spill over into the need to justify their clients' abuse as well.

Another example is that of marriage and family counselors. A counselor who is known to have a chronically troubled marriage, or a series of failed marriages, or extensive problems with his or her own children may be viewed as unsuccessful. Even though the experience gained in these relationships may be helpful to the counselor in guiding others, there are two potential problems here: One is that an individual's struggles may bias the ability to be objective and stimulate problems with countertransference. The other is a perception of relative personal ineptness in such matters, which may call the counselor's credibility into question.

Ultimately, helping professionals are free to make their own personal choices regarding their private lives. But they need to remember that these personal choices can have a profound impact on their professional lives as well.

Professional Competence

There are three major issues involved in ethical standards regarding professional competence:

1. Helping professionals have an ethical responsibility to make continuous efforts to improve their competence within their own professional specialty. There are two underlying philosophies here.

- One is a recognition that all such fields are dynamic, with new insights and techniques constantly discerned and old ones discarded. It is expected that professionals will accept the value of the experience and research of others, striving to stay abreast of current thinking in their field.
- · The other is that we are all ever-changing, fallible human beings, requiring continuing self-examination, education, and self-renewal.

Many organizations of helping professionals require regular participation in programs designed to enhance professional competence, often as a condition of continued licensure. Even when this is not the case, there is an ethical obligation to do so under this standard.

2. Helping professionals should not claim either directly or by implication credentials, training, or expertise they do not actually have; accept positions for which they are not actually qualified; or practice in specialties for which they have little or no training or professional experience.

Each professional specialty has its own discipline, techniques, and shared experiences that are applicable to it but often not to other specialties. Sometimes, in fact, procedures learned in one specialty can actually be harmful when applied to a client with a substantially different set of problems. Even when this is not the case, counselors in particular need to be cautious about straying into areas in which they have little or no professional training. When it develops that a client's problems go beyond a professional's own expertise, referral is always the better course than uninformed treatment.

The temptation for misrepresentation often increases as new areas of practice open up and competition for clients and work grows. It is important not to confuse personal interest or experiences, however valuable, with professional training and expertise.

3. Besides holding themselves to this ethical standard, ethical codes also require that helping professionals insist that others in their field do so, too. To do this, they must both confront failure on the part of peers to adhere to current standards of best practice and actively work to stop unqualified or unauthorized practice in their own field.

One important consideration here is that we have an ethical responsibility to ensure that the organizations we work for operate at high levels of competence. Employment by a specific organization means agreement by us with its standards and practices. Should this not be the case, we need to at least consider finding work elsewhere.

The appropriate sequence of behavior in such cases is:

1. Confront the appropriate individual in an effort to resolve the issue privately. In the case of an individual counselor who is acting unethically, the counselor should be confronted. Unethical behavior on the part of an organization should be addressed to those in the organization responsible for maintaining organizational standards.

2. In cases of individual problems concerning a colleague, if personal confrontation is unsuccessful, you should report your specific concerns to your supervisor. In especially severe cases (sexual involvement with a client, for example), you should inform your supervisor even if your colleague expresses a willingness to correct the problem. While this can present a dilemma in itself because of personal relationships and a need to be supportive of those we work with, it is sometimes necessary in order to protect clients from inappropriate behavior

and our organizations from legal action. In cases when the individual is not a colleague, or in cases in which organizational confrontation is unsuccessful—again if the violation is sufficiently severe—appropriate licensing or credentialing authorities should be informed.

3. Resign from a situation or job if a lack of resolution at any level reflects on your professional competence or the welfare of clients. This is important for personal as well as ethical reasons. Professionals are judged at least in part by the standards and practices of those they work for or with. And the organizations they work for and the individuals they work with are judged at least in part by their own standards and practices.

Finally, in order to work effectively within their own limits, helping professionals must have the personal maturity to judge themselves accurately, seeking feedback through appropriate colleagues or supervisors in order to assess their strengths, weaknesses, knowledge, and skills. And since insight without action is rarely beneficial, they must be willing to seek help when it is needed.

Professional Impairment

The importance of maintaining a healthy mind and unimpaired emotions is perhaps uniquely critical to the helping professional. Yet human difficulties such as chemical dependency, depression, and anxiety do not respect professional credentials. Many helping professionals seem to subscribe to a belief that they are (or should be) immune to such struggles because they are trained and called to help others. If they do recognize a problem in themselves, the adage "physician, heal thyself" often leaves them feeling weakened and diminished rather than challenged to positive action.

But a professional who is struggling with his or her own behavior may be unable to objectively assist another. It is human nature to judge another's experience within the context of our own. If, for example, a counselor lives in an abusive relationship, determined to make it work, he or she may unwittingly encourage clients to do the same. The defensive structure helpers erect to justify their own behavior may block their ability to recognize similar defenses in others.

It is vital that helping professionals continually monitor their own mental and physical health to ensure that they are not so impaired themselves that they are of little help to others and that they seek help when it is needed.

Unfortunately, often when it is recognized that a professional colleague has a problem, the response is criticism and gossip rather than confrontation and help. It is an important ethical mandate of the helping profession that members of it recognize the impact of impairment on the individual and the quality of service the individual provides, be willing to constructively confront difficulties within themselves and others, and work to provide the same compassionate and skillful assistance for impaired professionals that they offer to their clients. A safe environment for the treatment of helping professionals is important to the integrity of the profession.

Those who see impairment in colleagues should first discuss their observations privately with the colleague in a concerned and nonadversarial way. As is the case with clients, colleagues who are impaired often sense it and need confirmation from those they respect before seeking help. If this intervention is unsuccessful, the situation should be called to the attention of a supervisor.

It should be noted that failure to confront such problems puts the professional who knows of them but does not act on this knowledge in the position of enabling a difficult situation to worsen, often putting both the impaired professional and clients at risk. This could have both ethical and serious legal consequences.

Nondiscrimination

All ethical standards say that helping professionals have a personal ethical responsibility to provide their services to all who seek them, regardless of either their clients' or their own race, religion, age, sex, handicaps, national ancestry, sexual orientation, or (to the extent that we can control this) economic condition. This goes beyond assuring availability of services; it extends to the provision of services of equal competence, quality, and relevance.

While nondiscrimination is for most helping professionals an important personal ethical principle, in practice it can sometimes present problems. Like all other human beings, helping professionals have their own personal biases and, in some cases, prejudices. But the ban on discrimination in providing their services is found in all professional ethical standards and should be observed, not only because of the professional requirement but because it is the right thing to do. In this respect, helping professionals need to remember that it is frequently in the treatment of clients who present them with the most difficulty that they receive the most knowledge and—ultimately—satisfaction.

Particularly in therapeutic relationships, the practice of nondiscrimination can be subtle and complex. It requires rigorous review by counselors and therapists of their work and self-examination in order to ensure adherence to this important principle.

There are, of course, occasions in which a bias is so strong that it cannot be overcome. If this is the case and poor or improper treatment is the result, the obvious answer is referral to another professional. Care should be taken, however, in resorting to this course of action. The easiest way to deal with a difficult client is to refer the client to another counselor on the grounds of inability to provide effective treatment. This should be avoided whenever possible, and supervisors should discourage it when there is no overwhelming reason for a referral.

The prohibition against discrimination on economic grounds can be particularly troublesome. The fact is that lots of men, women, and children in need of and seeking help—perhaps especially in need of mental and behavioral health treatment—are denied it every day for economic reasons that are inherently discriminatory according to most ethical standards. That is, they have no money to pay for treatment, and public treatment facilities are often limited. Thus treatment is frequently denied in direct violation of this principle.

From the point of view of most helping professionals, however, the prohibition of discrimination on economic grounds applies only to the actions of the individual professional acting as an individual and not necessarily to the organizations for which the professional works. Even so, it is important for helping professionals to confront inequities within their organizations. Those who work for organizations that charge fees for their services should work within their organizations to provide free or low-fee services to the needy to the extent that resources are available to do so, or to provide a referral service to organizations that provide similar services at lower cost.

Professionals who work within organizations are not required by this principle to provide no- or below-cost services when they have no control over fees charged for their work. But it is an important part of their responsibilities to help society understand the need to provide treatment services to all who can benefit from them.

Private practitioners in single or group practice who do control their own fee structures, however, should also take careful note of this requirement and fulfill it. Some private practitioners earmark a percentage of their time for no- or low-pay clients. Many have a sliding fee scale based on clients' relative abilities to pay. Others, when faced with potential clients who do not have the ability to pay their normal fees, refer them to practitioners or agencies that can provide good treatment at lower cost. The major issue here is to ensure that proper treatment is given or services provided to all who need them.

Cultural Competence

Helping professionals who serve a diverse group of clients have an ethical responsibility to reach beyond general competence in their specialty to cultural competence in understanding and treating the specific cultural needs of their clients.

Often clients have little in common with each other except the fact that they all need help. And often, too, they have little in common with the people who help them. Sometimes these differences are relatively minor, but at other times they can be so significant that they stand in the way of satisfactory outcomes if they are not successfully addressed. This is especially true for those who work for publicly supported agencies, which typically have a highly diverse client base.

All individuals bring to their work the reality of their own lives, based on race, ethnic heritage, gender, age, sexual orientation, and other aspects of their own individuality. If these differences are not understood and acknowledged in a professional relationship with those we want to help, very little can be accomplished.

Cultural competence goes beyond "political correctness," and even cultural sensitivity, and recognizes that words have different meanings in different cultures, as do body language, ways of addressing problems, worldviews, and other factors related to assessment, treatment, and providing needed and useful services. For examples:

• Women are much more likely than men to acknowledge mental health problems and seek help for them. Women are also much more likely than men to have poverty-connected problems since they are far more likely than men to have responsibility for their children as well as for themselves.

• A lack of cultural competence by some mental health professionals can have a significant negative impact on African Americans. A 1995 needs assessment prepared for the Hamilton County (Ohio) Community Mental Health Board reported that in Ohio, for example, African Americans constitute 10% of the total population but represent 36% of annual admissions to state psychiatric hospitals; are four times more likely than whites to be involuntarily admitted to a state psychiatric hospital; and are far more likely than whites to be readmitted to state hospitals within the same year they are discharged.

While there may well be other reasons for these discrepancies, the report said, those who looked at the issue closely concluded that the most significant reason was a lack of cultural competence on the part of those professionals—mostly white—who assessed African Americans' mental health and made choices about the level at which they needed treatment.

• Gay men and lesbians also face problems getting help because of a lack of cultural understanding by heterosexual professionals. Obviously some of this is the result of homophobia.

But some professionals who do not consider themselves homophobic and would like to help gay clients have difficulty doing so successfully because of a lack of understanding of gay cultural norms, particularly in respect to sexual issues and feelings of isolation and discrimination.

These are but three of many examples of special populations with special needs who require help by professionals who are culturally competent to provide it. We can also add the growing number of elderly in our society who will need counselors who are geriatrically competent. The list goes on and on.

Some members of cultural groups say that they can be successfully helped only by another member of their culture. But most agree that cultural competence that includes empathy, needed special skills, and, perhaps most important, self-awareness on the part of the helper of his or her own limitations and biases is sufficient. To this list should be added a willingness on the part of professionals who do not have sufficient training to provide culturally competent help to admit this fact at the beginning of a professional relationship and let the client decide whether to continue. It should also be noted that simply sharing a cultural background does not necessarily guarantee cultural competence.

Fees

Although clients' interests and ability to pay should be given consideration in the setting of fees, community and professional ethical standards safeguard the financial interests of the individual professional. That is, while a client's ability to pay must be taken into consideration when establishing a fee, the individual professional has an ethical right to charge a fee that is reasonable by the standards of the community and the profession.

Thus, helping professionals who have the ability to set their own fees should do so with the client's ability to pay in mind, charge enough to ensure that they can afford to continue to work in their profession, and avoid all situations in which their personal gain might undermine the client's right to economically fair treatment.

As noted earlier, the responsibilities of treatment agencies, hospitals, and the community to provide services regardless of an individual's ability to pay are not addressed by the ethical codes for individual counselors. These codes apply only to those professionals who have the ability to set their own fees or establish a fee based on their employers' flexible fee schedule.

But whether or not they have the ability to set their own fees, professionals have an obligation to keep a client informed of alternative services within the community that may meet his or her needs more economically, even if doing so may deprive the professional or employer of revenue.

On the other hand, helping professionals and their employers have a right to receive a reasonable fee for their work. Thus, while they have an obligation to inform clients when lower cost services of similar quality exist, they have no obligation to urge these services on a client who can pay a reasonable fee for treatment. Also, in some cases, lower cost treatment may not fully meet an individual client's needs. When this is the case, it should be pointed out.

Under no circumstances are helping professionals to accept gifts, commissions, kickbacks or rebates for referral of clients to a particular program or counselor, nor are they to make barter arrangements with clients in which they provide services in return for work. (These issues are discussed in Chapter 5, in the section on business involvement in "Dual Relationships.")

In addition, it is important to accurately represent fees and/or other reimbursements to third-party funders, such as insurance companies. For example, it is both unethical and illegal to waive a client's co-payment without permission from the insurance company paying the claim. It is also unethical to charge the insured a higher fee than that charged to uninsured clients.

Finally on this subject, it is unethical to change fee arrangements during the course of therapy unless notice of a possible impending change has been given at the onset of treatment.

Community and Society

Expertise gained through training and experience in their own specialty often gives helping professionals a special standing in and responsibility to society as a source of objective information about what they do and the problems they treat.

One specific ethical responsibility professionals have to society is to help broaden and deepen the level of understanding among the general public of the special problems they deal with professionally. Mental health professionals, for example, have the responsibility to help keep the public informed about mental illnesses and developments in their treatment. Substance abuse counselors have the responsibility to help keep the public informed about treatment effectiveness and opportunities. Each specialty has its own responsibility in this respect.

As a corollary, helping professionals should help form and be advocates for public policies that positively impact the type of clients they work with. Perhaps chief among the public policies helping professionals should advocate is making sure services such as those they offer are available to all who need them, regardless of economic circumstances.

Professionals who work for organizations need to take care in those cases in which their views are not endorsed by their employer, and especially in those cases in which their views and their employer's are at odds. In these cases, they should make it clear that their comments are those of an individual professional rather than that of the organization by which they're employed. When they're taking a public position at odds with that of their employer, they should notify their employer that they plan to do so, and tell their audience in what way the two positions are different.

It should be noted that there are legal limitations on the extent to which public service and tax-exempt organizations may use their resources—including their human resources—to support or oppose specific legislative initiatives. And many agencies have restrictions on who may speak officially for them.

Colleagues

1. Most ethical codes require helping professionals to cooperate with colleagues in their own and other specialties to advance professional interests and meet common concerns. In doing so, they should treat all colleagues with respect, fairness, and courtesy, remembering that ethical prohibitions against discrimination refer to all those with whom they deal professionally, and not only to their clients.

2. Professionals have an ethical responsibility to respect confidences shared with them professionally and to represent accurately and fairly colleagues' views when it is appropriate to do so. All professionals need a feeling of safety within their own organizations and among their own peers so that they may express themselves freely and without fear of inappropriate negative consequences.

3. Should a professional replace or be replaced by a colleague in professional practice, it is especially important that she or he at all times behave in a way that will give full consideration to the interest, character, and reputation of that colleague.

4. Professionals should be careful not to exploit a conflict with a colleague, or between a colleague and his or her employer or client, to advance their own interests. And when they have serious professional disputes with a colleague, they should seek arbitration or mediation by mutual peers.

5. Professionals should not solicit clients of colleagues.

6. Should professionals assume responsibility for a client of another professional or agency, they have the responsibility to notify the counselor or agency that they have done so. When they take temporary responsibility for a client of another counselor, they should treat this client with the same degree of professionalism and consideration given regular clients.

Profession

Helping professionals have an ethical responsibility to act in ways that maintain and advance the values and standards of their profession and the way in which it is perceived by the public. This responsibility goes beyond their own responsibility to perform at a high level of competence. It also requires them to work to increase the overall knowledge in and quality of their profession as well as utilizing appropriate channels (discussed in "Professional Competence") to work against shoddy, unethical practices and unqualified practices by others in their profession.

Those who work in helping professions need to be ever mindful of the fact that each of them to a large extent represents their entire profession to those with whom they work. At the same time, they are defined at least in part by the overall reputation of their profession. This means that when they believe that their profession is routinely engaging in practices that are not in the best interests of society, they need to take appropriate steps to bring about change.

Employers

Helping professionals have an ethical responsibility to honor their commitments to their employers. They must also adhere to both the letter and spirit of work rules and codes of practice adopted by their organizations, so long as these are consistent with good ethical and clinical practices. (What to do when they are not consistent is discussed in "Professional Competence.")

In this connection, helping professionals have an ethical responsibility to work with their employers in efforts to improve the effectiveness of programs and the efficiency, policies, and procedures under which they operate, always within appropriate channels.

Additionally, of course, they have the obligation common to all employees to refrain from treating the resources of their employers as though they were their own. This means, among other things, limiting personal phone calls and not charging personal long-distance calls to the organization's account and buying rather than appropriating office supplies when they are for personal use.

Ethical Dilemmas for Discussion and Resolution

The authors' suggestions for resolving these dilemmas are in Chapter 12.

1. I am a social worker employed by a county social service agency. I'm clean and sober during the week, but on weekends, we (the man I live with and some of our friends) sometimes drink pretty heavily and do drugs on occasion. Once or twice things have gotten out of hand and the police have been called. Nothing came of this, but I'm beginning to get worried about what might happen to my job if I get picked up for being under the influence or in possession of a proscribed substance. Is this an ethical issue? It does not affect my performance in any way.

2. I work for a social service agency that seems constantly to be chasing dollars. That is, it looks to me as though when the people who run the place find out about the possibility of a grant for offering a specific kind of treatment, they claim to have people on staff who are qualified to do the work, but they actually don't. Then when they get the grant, they run around trying to hire the people they claimed to have, or try to make those of us who have different kinds of training offer the treatment they're being paid to deliver. I'm sure this is an ethical violation on their part. Is it? What should I do about it?

3. I am a substance abuse counselor, and most of my clients are women who have substance abuse problems to a varying degree. I know all of the warning signs of drug dependence, and I'm pretty well free of them myself, but there are times when things get too much for me and I go off and get drunk, usually by myself. This doesn't happen often, but it does happen often enough so that I'm aware of it. Sometimes when I'm discussing with a client her use of drugs, I find myself downplaying my feelings about how much she's using because it seems to match my own behavior. Do I have an ethical problem here?

4. I'm a heterosexual therapist, and an increasing number of my clients are gay. This is often not apparent until we get into the treatment process, and I stumble onto it when they bring up sexual or relationship issues that are beyond my own experience and training. I don't consider myself homophobic, and the issues they bring up don't shock me particularly. It's just that I think I have too little knowledge of gay cultural norms to offer them much help, and I suspect they think that, too. Ethically, what should I do in this kind of situation?

5. I work in a treatment facility that seems to routinely discharge clients when their insurance or money runs out rather than when they're ready for discharge. Yet I know that the ethical standards of my profession require me to give needed treatment regardless of an individual's economic circumstances. Does this mean I'm supposed to provide free treatment? What should I do?

6. My supervisor has asked me to sign discharge papers for someone I know needs at least one more week of treatment. I'm sure the reason for the discharge is that the client's insurance has run out and he can't afford to pay for additional treatment himself. What are my ethical responsibilities here?

7. I work in a residential child care facility with someone I can't stand either personally or professionally. I think he is arrogant, has lots of problems dealing with women, and pretends to have far more expertise than he actually has. There is a vacancy in another agency for a much better job, and both he and I have applied for it. I'm qualified and convinced that he isn't. Don't I have an ethical responsibility to point out his lack of qualifications to the person who will be doing the hiring?

8. I think there are lots of ways in which the agency I work with could provide better service to our clients. I'm a therapeutic aide, which puts me pretty far down on the food chain here, and I'm not sure anyone above me has much interest in what I have to say about it. Are there any ethical requirements that tell me what I should do about this?

9. I work full time in a social service agency for very little pay. I've been offered a part-time job running a program for another agency. I have a family to support, and the salary from my full-time job doesn't go very far. If I work some evenings and patch together vacation time and sick time due to me from my full-time job, I could do what would be required of me on the other job. Would this be unethical?

THE ETHICAL DILEMMA RESOLUTION WORKSHEET

Use this form as a guide when resolving each ethical dilemma. Doing so is a good way to ensure that all steps are taken to reach a satisfactory decision.

1. The ethical standard or principle involved

2. Ethical trap possibilities

3. Preliminary response

4. Possible consequences of adopting this response

5. Ethical resolution

CHAPTER 5

Client Welfare and Client Relationships

The Ethical Standards

The protection and enhancement of long-term client welfare is paramount in the client/counselor relationship. This relationship requires the following ethical conduct:

- Making self-reliance, freedom of choice, and self-determination on the part of each client a major counseling goal; beginning each counseling relationship with a discussion of the client's right to know about the counseling techniques used and the limitations and objectives of counseling
- Carefully monitoring counseling effectiveness and terminating relationships that are not effective after a reasonable amount of time
- Terminating relationships in a way that protects the interests of the client
- Fully disclosing any secondary uses of the client relationship, such as use of the client or treatment in research, taping counseling or treatment sessions, special supervision, and the professional's own biases in treatment methods
- Ensuring maximum physical and emotional safety for the client throughout the relationship, including the client's participation in group therapy and role play
- Prompt notification and resolution of issues when more than one practitioner is involved in a client's treatment
- Understanding of and adherence to special requirements regarding the treatment of children and those who are legally unable to make their own decisions
- Rejecting or discouraging gifts from clients
- Refraining from all forms of dual relationships with clients, including emotional, sexual, and business involvement

Helping professionals—especially those who are counselors and therapists—have a unique and uniquely intimate relationship with their clients.

Successful treatment always requires a high degree of trust on the part of the client as well as competence on the part of the professional, and this trust must not be broken by the professional. In order to preserve this trust, professionals need to acknowledge and fully understand that they are, within the scope of their professional relationships, responsible for protecting the welfare of the clients with whom they work, whether working with them as individuals or as members of a group.

In part, this means that they must give each client the benefit of the best of their professional abilities and do so with respect for them as individuals.

It also means that professionals must be careful to ensure that they do nothing to advance their own personal needs at the financial or emotional expense of their clients. Although there are many aspects to this relationship, those regarding dual relationships—professional and personal—are particularly sensitive.

Self-Reliance, Freedom of Choice, and Self-Determination

Maximizing freedom of choice and self-determination on the part of each client is a key ethical as well as a clinical objective.

Therapeutic purposes, goals, techniques, procedures, limitations, and confidentiality rights and limitations should be carefully spelled out and discussed with each client before treatment begins. In therapeutic situations, the client should be made aware of any relevant theoretical orientation held by the counselor and the effect this may have on his or her approach to problem solving and therapeutic goals. Once this information has been presented and discussed, the client should be asked to consent to the kind of treatment discussed. In all cases except those involving clients who are legally unable to act on their own behalf, clients should be informed that they have the right to refuse certain types of treatment, even when the professional believes the treatment is appropriate.

Effectiveness

Despite the popular mandate "when in doubt, do no harm," a neutral outcome in therapeutic counseling is not enough. What therapists do professionally is expected to be helpful and they should work out minimum standards for progress with each client and end any relationship that is not at least meeting these goals over a reasonable period of time. When it is necessary to terminate a relationship for this reason, it is important to make sure the client understands the reasons for the termination and to refer the client to one or more other professionals who might provide a more effective fit.

Adequate supervisory relationships and quality assurance measures within organizations offer the professional a way of evaluating effectiveness on a regular basis. Those working on their own should seek out professional relationships that offer an opportunity for objective review of their work.

As noted elsewhere, effectiveness can also be limited because of cultural differences or value clashes; not every professional can work effectively with everyone who walks in the door. Again, however, alternatives need to be suggested.

Termination

Because of the intimate nature of therapeutic relationships and the trust clients have in their counselors, when professionals choose to terminate a professional relationship they need to do so with care and full consideration of the client's best interests. Except under very unusual circumstances (such as the personal safety of the counselor or the sudden termination of the counselor's employment, for example), it is unethical to end such a relationship precipitously.

Every effort should be made to provide continuity of treatment by a single helping professional. It is inappropriate to refer a client to another professional simply because the client has become difficult for one reason or another. Difficult clients often give professionals a greater opportunity to learn and grow than do easier ones. Sometimes, though, it is necessary to transfer a client to another professional. Some of the reasons for this include reassignment of the professional, promotion, resignation, or lack of progress. When this is necessary, it must be done carefully and thoughtfully, and in full consultation with the client. The situation should be discussed with the client fully and openly, recognizing that a change may appear threatening to a client.

Two key points to keep in mind are:

1. All professionals should be sufficiently knowledgeable about alternative helpers—or at least where they can be found—to be able to make a satisfactory referral.
2. A counselor or therapist who must terminate a client relationship may do so even if the client refuses a reasonable referral.

Some believe that more clients are damaged by therapists who will not let them terminate than by those who terminate too quickly. It is important to be mindful of whose needs are being met in extended therapeutic relationships. It is unethical to keep clients in treatment primarily because they pay regularly or are interesting or attractive.

Disclosures

There are to be no hidden agendas when working with a client. Full disclosure of taping, use of the client in research, the nature and extent of supervision, and so on are all to be disclosed to clients so that they may choose for themselves their level of participation, if any. This requirement includes disclosure of the professional's own biases with regard to treatment or service delivery methods.

Client Emotional Safety

Professionals have an ethical responsibility to preserve and protect the emotional safety of their clients. Clients trust the professionals they work with to apply their knowledge of the client and the relative risks involved in various treatment methods and use only those that are likely to ensure this safety. For the most part, these decisions are clinical rather than ethical, but two examples of a need for special care are pointed out in many ethical standards, especially for counselors and therapists. They are:

Group Therapy

Group therapy which encourages self-disclosure and self-examination, needs to be carefully organized and conducted with primary consideration given to clients' interests and especially to clients' emotional safety. Those professionals who organize therapeutic groups should carefully screen prospective group members to ensure compatibility and freedom from physical or emotional danger.

Professionals who run groups need to be alert to protect clients' emotional safety from excessively judgmental statements from other members of groups in which they are participants.

Additionally, groups should be reminded regularly of the confidential nature of what they learn about others during sessions. Few things can injure a group participant more, or destroy a group faster, than knowledge that others in the group are talking about members' problems with outsiders. Those group members who do violate the group's confidentiality should be asked immediately to leave the group.

Cultural and value differences among group members and between the group leaders and members of the group can affect both safety and effectiveness. In general, culturally diverse groups should be encouraged since they provide an opportunity for a range of insights and personal growth by all participants who learn from one another. There are circumstances, though, in which culturally "different" individuals can be damaged by thoughtless comments made by others who don't share or understand these differences.

In our experience, for example, many gay people who want and would benefit from group therapy are reluctant to join groups predominately made up of heterosexuals working on the same therapeutic problems because of fear of ridicule. In cases like this, emotional safety issues stand in the way of successful therapy.

Careful screening of all those invited to join a particular group to ensure compatibility and appropriate disclosures to all about the nature of the specific group and discussions about it are part of the answer. Vigilance on the part of the group's facilitator is another.

Role Playing

Professionals need to recognize that client participation in therapy involving role playing or classroom or other training demonstrations can be emotionally dangerous to the client. To avoid potential damage, professionals and their clients must carefully judge how the experience will impact on the client after the event. It is easy to forget that clients often want to please their helpers and will generally agree to anything they think might benefit helpers or their programs. This should not be taken advantage of. Even when using other professionals in a training demonstration, careful consideration must be given by all concerned to the potential impact.

Multiple Treatment

Treatment of clients by more than one professional at a time raises some ethical and practical issues that need discussion.

For example, different practitioners may have different treatment methods, and the client's welfare can be jeopardized by real or perceived conflicts among them. Therefore, it is in the client's best interest that if he or she is seeing more than one practitioner, all involved are made aware of this fact.

A counselor or therapist should find out in the initial interview with a prospective client whether she or he is also receiving treatment from another professional, and for what. In those cases in which other treatment is being given, all parties, including the client, should determine to what extent multiple treatment is appropriate. Be aware that the client must give written permission to all professionals involved before a discussion of treatment alternatives may take place. Professionals discussing this issue with other professionals need to share their opinions about assessment of the client and his or her needs, agree on priorities of desired outcomes, and, if multiple treatment is thought necessary, make sure each professional understands the treatment methods of the others.

An additional consideration is that many individuals being treated for mental illnesses are also abusers of alcohol and other drugs and seek treatment for this illness, too. While it is not necessarily likely that the two treatments will actually be in conflict, it is possible that mentally ill clients will read conflicts into different treatment methods and either become confused or play off one practitioner against another.

Besides learning if another professional is involved in the client's treatment, substance abuse counselors in particular need to find out in the initial interview if the client is taking any medications and if so, what they are for. Some professionals treating chemically addicted clients for forms of mental illness will ignore the addiction and prescribe addictive drugs to treat the symptoms of the mental illness. It is not at all unusual, for example, for therapists or physicians treating drug-addicted clients for anxiety to prescribe tranquilizers or other addictive antianxiety drugs. Substance abuse counselors need to be alert to this and work with the client and the other professionals involved to establish treatment priorities. There is no point in trying to treat a client's drug abuse while the client is routinely taking an addictive drug prescribed by another professional for another illness.

In order to protect both the client and the professionals involved, it is far better for the counselor to notify other involved professionals about multiple involvement than to leave this to the client (after receiving written permission for such discussion from the client). In the disclosure process, all relevant information about treatment—including medication—should be discussed.

Additionally, counselors need to find out what kind of support groups and other forms of self-help therapies the client is using. Counseling in combination with self-help programs can be powerfully helpful to the client. However, counselors and therapists need to keep abreast of the kind of advice their clients are getting and from whom.

In general, practitioners should be skeptical about the advisability of multiple therapies and work out with the client a system of priorities for the treatment of one problem at a time.

Minors and Those Legally Unable to Make Their Own Decisions

Both ethical standards and the law guide decision making about minors and individuals legally declared incompetent to make their own decisions. While these are obviously two different populations, ethical requirements regarding them as clients are essentially similar.

Legal Issues

It should be noted at the outset that regardless of ethical considerations, treating both minors and those legally unable to make their own decisions without parental or guardian consent in most cases is illegal. And, especially in the case of minors, gaining consent can sometimes be difficult. In the vast majority of cases in which consent for treatment cannot be obtained, it should not be given. Exceptions are in the few states that allow counseling of individuals 12 years of age or older without parental consent in cases that involve possible harm to the child or others, or in cases of child abuse or incest.

Should the helping professional believe that consent for treatment is being withheld inappropriately, recourse is often available through child welfare agencies in the case of children or probate courts in the case of legally incompetent adults.

Additionally, particularly in respect to minors, it is important to remember that there is a legal distinction between education and treatment. That is, it may be lawful to inform (educate) a minor client about various pitfalls in pursuing certain courses of action and about lifestyle alternatives in cases when consent for treatment is withheld or otherwise unavailable.

Information Sharing

For the most part, parents and guardians have the right to know what is being said and learned in counseling sessions. It is important that clients understand this to the extent that they are capable of so that the practitioner is not accused of breaching trust. Trust can be maintained through careful and prudent record keeping and careful consideration about exactly what information needs to be shared.

In order to protect the interests of all parties—including the client, the parents/guardians, and the practitioner—a thorough and honest discussion of expectations of both what specific information will be shared and the potential outcomes of treatment should take place before treatment begins.

Many ethical dilemmas and legal problems in this area could be headed off by the development of a three-way contract signed by all parties in which the details of what will and will not be revealed are spelled out.

Finally, with both minors and those declared incompetent, what may be the most important thing to remember is the ethical requirement to keep the clients' interests first when sharing information, rather than those of parents or guardians.

Substance Abuse Counselors

As is the case with the confidentiality issues discussed in Chapter 6, substance abuse counselors need to be aware of special legal considerations that apply to them but not to those in other counseling specialties. In keeping with the spirit of federal laws allowing alcoholics and other drug addicts to seek treatment without fear of repercussions, over half the states have specific statutes allowing the treatment of minors for chemical dependencies, including alcohol, without parental consent. In some of these states, however, though consent is not required, notification of parents that treatment is taking place is. In those states that still require parental/guardian consent for the chemical abuse treatment of minors, the minor must sign a consent form before his or her parents are notified.

Some of this is very tricky stuff. Clear understanding of legal obligations may require the assistance of an experienced colleague or attorney.

Court-Ordered Treatment

An increasing number of individuals are becoming clients of mental health and substance abuse treatment agencies by court order. That is, they are ordered to receive treatment at a specific facility either as part of a jail sentence or in lieu of one. In most cases, if the clients leave treatment before they are supposed to, they must complete the jail sentence that was the alternative to treatment. Such clients are legally wards of the court that sent them to the treatment facility. Parole and probation officers generally stand in for the court in these circumstances and are legal guardians of the client regardless of the client's age. Although the courts, rather than parents or guardians, have legal responsibility in such cases, many facilities that offer such treatment to juvenile offenders also report progress to parents and hold regular sessions with them during treatment as a way of making them a positive part of the stabilization or recovery program. Similar treatment is often given to spouses or significant others in cases involving adult clients.

Gifts

What to do about gifts from clients is a problem that plagues many helping professionals. In general, it is unethical to accept gifts from clients. As with other delicate issues, it is best to have a policy that is made clear to clients at the start. In the absence of this, a realistic assessment of the motivation behind the gift and the value of the gift needs to be made.

It is essential to view all gifts from clients as meaningful in the context of the client relationship; the act of both offering and acceptance or rejection of a gift will carry meaning beyond the gift itself. It is important not to injure the client's self-esteem by the rigid rejection of small gifts.

In the case of small gifts or tokens, the culture of the professional organization or community should be taken into consideration. In residential settings, for instance, clients often present their counselors and other professionals with arts and crafts projects made while in treatment. If this is the norm, and it does not seem to reflect complex transference or manipulation, acceptance may be ethical and rejection may be inappropriate.

Many counselors resolve the problem by sharing all gifts with the agency or other professionals involved in their practice. For example, a gift of flowers or food can be shared with all. Clients who insist on giving gifts of money beyond their fees can make a donation to the organization helping them or to another that needs financial support.

Dual Relationships

Professional relationships with individuals who are also close emotionally, socially, or in business are filled with potential ethical problems and must be avoided. It stands to reason that given the delicacy of such relationships, professionals should refrain from treating people when their emotional involvement could cloud their judgment or inhibit their clients. This is especially true of family members, close friends, or others with whom the professional might have a vested interest. Even professional relationships with friends of friends can present difficulties, especially for counselors and therapists, and should be avoided.

Appropriate refusal to provide treatment or other services to relatives and friends may also protect both client and professional from casual meetings in social situations. When such meetings do accidentally occur, the best course of action on the part of the professional is to let the client take the lead. That is, if the client initiates a conversation or introduces the professional to others, the professional must allow the client to state the dimensions of the relationship, or even if one exists.

Sexual Involvement

It is clearly unethical for a helping professional to engage in sexual activity with a client. This prohibition is explicitly mentioned in every professional code of ethics. But while this ban is unambiguous, some questions remain. For example, who is a client, and what is sexual activity?

Who is a client? Many organizations answer this question for the professional by insisting that the professional refrain from personal contact with "clients" for a certain length of time (or forever) and/or by considering all clients of the organization to be clients of all its professionals. The best rule of thumb for a counselor or therapist is never to engage in sexual activity with someone whom he or she has ever treated or who has been treated by his or her agency. It is also unethical to terminate a professional relationship in order to start a personal one.

Note that this prohibition against sexual involvement is not dependent on who initiates it. It is always the responsibility of the helping professional to manage the client/therapist relationship, including its boundaries.

When we think of sexual activity, we often think only of intercourse. But other kinds of sexual behavior fall under this prohibition as well, including seductive or sexualized behavior. For example, helping professionals need to pay attention to any indiscriminate touching and hugging on their or their clients' part. While most such expressions of affection are innocent on the part of the initiator, the professional needs to be concerned with how they may be perceived by the recipient.

Sexual harassment is a form of sexual involvement that is clearly unethical. This goes beyond unwelcome efforts to force sexual intercourse and extends to language with a sexual content and, of course, to body contact. This is an increasingly charged issue and the intimacy of virtually every care-giving relationship carries with it some potential dangers. These potential dangers need to be recognized by the practitioner since the client is often incapable of doing so.

Those who feel a strong sexual attraction to a client should consider this feeling to be damaging to the therapeutic relationship as well as to themselves professionally and should consult with a skilled and mature professional. The imbalance of power between therapist and client is so clear that one important question that should be discussed in such a consultation is, "Why am I so attracted to someone who is—at least by definition—emotionally weaker than I am?"

Business Involvement

In general, it is not ethically appropriate to engage in business dealings with clients. It is unrealistic to assume that the client and the professional can keep the two relationships totally separate and at arm's length. All interactions between a client and the person who is helping her or him have meaning to the client. In considering a business arrangement with a client, no matter how trivial it may seem, a professional needs to consider the possible result of a negative as well as a positive outcome. It is very possible that the professional's criticism of the client's performance in the business relationship may damage the therapeutic relationship.

On the other hand, practitioners also need to exercise some common sense. If, for example, a helping professional needs the services of a tree-trimmer following a severe storm and the only tree-trimmer in town is a client, the practitioner may use the client's services. But when it is necessary to do business with a client, three things must be ensured:

1. All the normal standards and procedures of both businesses and professions must be followed. That is, the work done must be neither more nor less satisfactory than that done for others, and the fee charged must be the same as the fee charged others for the same work.
2. The nature of the professional/client relationship must be kept confidential.
3. Compensation for the work must be in money rather than services; barter arrangements are fraught with ethical problems.

Ethical Dilemmas for Discussion and Resolution

The authors' suggestions for resolution of these dilemmas are in Chapter 12.

1. I am a case worker in a mental health agency. One of the clients assigned to me has expressed his "love" for me and has recently said something to the effect that if he can't have me, no one will. He has never acted out on any of this, but what he says makes me very uneasy. I've talked with my supervisor about this from time to time, but she says we're way understaffed—which we are—and that reshuffling assignments would be difficult. Also, in her opinion I'm doing a good job with this client and she thinks that abruptly changing this relationship might be bad for the client. What are my ethical responsibilities?

2. I am a therapist and have been treating a client regularly for several years. I think the usefulness of the therapeutic relationship is over. That is, I've taken her about as far as I can and she seems to be using me as a crutch to help her out when she should be walking by herself. I've been leading her toward the idea of termination fairly firmly, but without any effect. I've talked this over with my supervisor, who makes the point that continuing to see her is probably not doing her any harm, plus, she says, my client is one of the few we have who pays the full fee and does so on time. What should I do?

3. I am counseling a young woman—she's 15—who is very active sexually. I have regular meetings with her mother to talk about her daughter's therapy and issues. Her mother clearly has no idea about what her daughter is up to, and I'm not sure ethically whether I should tell her about it or keep it to myself. What should I do?

4. This same young woman tells me that she's pregnant and asks me for advice about what to do. I think she ought to have an abortion, but I'm not sure that ethically that's what I should tell her. Is it? What should I do?

5. Should I tell the mother that her daughter's pregnant?

6. I work in an agency that helps individuals with mental disabilities, many of whom are institutionalized. One of my clients, who has a severe mental disability and lives in a residential home, leads me to believe that he is being sexually abused by at least one

member of the staff. I'm not really sure about this because it's difficult to separate fact from fantasy when talking with him about other things. What should I do?

7. I am an activities therapist and one of my clients was divorced recently. We discuss his marital problems fairly frequently, and I feel that I understand his former wife very well. She called me the other day to talk about him and his treatment, which I told her I couldn't do. The conversation turned flirtatious, and we made a date for drinks. Before things go too far, are there any ethical requirements about how far I can take this?

8. One of my clients keeps coming on to me. She tells me she usually wears beat-up old clothes and takes little interest in her appearance, but every time she comes in, it looks like she's just come from the beauty parlor, she's wearing a new dress, and all the rest. She's made several comments about her sexual needs, which should probably be explored in the course of our therapy, but I'm reluctant to because I'm not sure where it would go. What are the ethical considerations I need to be thinking about?

9. I'm a facilitator of a group of emotionally disturbed adolescents. A couple of them have a lot of trouble with boundaries, especially involving me. They take every opportunity to hug and touch me before and after the group meets and throw all sorts of sexual innuendoes my way. I'm concerned that if I say anything about this, it will harm the therapeutic relationship. But I'm also concerned about the situation if I let it go on. What should I do ethically?

10. I mentioned the fact that I'm going to be moving to another apartment in a couple of weeks to a client. Now he seems to have taken this on as his own move, offering me a truck and his help in loading and unloading it. He seems sincere and I really need the help. May I accept it from him?

11. The hairdresser I've been going to for several years has been hinting that she has some emotional problems. Now she's shown up at my agency and wants to become my client. May I accept her as a client? If I do, can she still do my hair?

12. I am a substance abuse counselor who has a client with a lot of marital problems as well as his substance abuse problem. He tends to blame his drinking on his marital problems and wants to set up a session in which I see both him and his wife together so that I can help him make her understand his point of view. While I certainly don't think his wife is responsible for his drinking, if what he says about her behavior is anywhere near accurate, I think they could clearly use some marital counseling. Is it okay ethically for me to provide this service?

13. I am a counselor and one of my clients seems to resist treatment. She gets right to the edge of confronting her problems and then steps back. One of my colleagues is running a therapeutic weekend for people with her kind of problems. It is quite intense and I believe participating might jump-start her therapy in a way that one-on-one counseling doesn't seem to. I've talked with her about it and she seems reluctant, but I'm sure I can convince her. What are my ethical responsibilities?

14. One of my co-workers is a therapist who has told me that he feels a strong sexual attraction to one of his clients. We have discussed the dangers and implications of this several times, and he seems to be aware of them. But I can't be sure of what he's going to do. Having a sexual relationship with a client would clearly be an ethical violation that could involve my agency as well as him. Do I have an ethical requirement to report this to our supervisor?

THE ETHICAL DILEMMA RESOLUTION WORKSHEET

Use this form as a guide when resolving each ethical dilemma. Doing so is a good way to ensure that all steps are taken to reach a satisfactory decision.

1. The ethical standard or principle involved

2. Ethical trap possibilities

3. Preliminary response

4. Possible consequences of adopting this response

5. Ethical resolution

CHAPTER 6

Confidentiality

The Ethical Standards

Helping professionals must respect the privacy of clients and take all reasonable and legal measures to ensure it both while the helping relationship is active and after it has been terminated. This includes:

- Preserving the confidentiality of treatment sessions
- Maintaining, storing, and exchanging records and other information in a way that protects client privacy both during and after treatment
- Understanding the uses and limitations of waivers of confidentiality and informed consent statements
- Understanding state and federal privacy laws as they relate to both privacy in general and the specific requirements that apply to some helping profession specialties
- Understanding the ethical and legal qualifications to confidentiality standards—when confidential information *must* and when it *may* be disclosed to others

Confidentiality is among the most important traditions of the helping professions. This is because only those who feel sufficiently safe in a professional relationship will divulge and discuss the most sensitive aspects of their lives. They cannot do so if they fear that this information may be used in a way that could harm them. This high degree of safety can be ensured only if the professional makes it clear to each client that confidentiality will be maintained and then adheres to the letter and spirit of this ethical principle.

However, important—and in some cases obvious—as these ethical requirements are, as helping professionals we need to be aware that there is both more and less to the confidentiality issue than may at first be apparent. There's more involved because of the fact that in some instances federal and state laws may at least seem to require different behavior on the part of professionals than do their ethical standards. And there's less involved because in some cases clients may have less privacy protection in legal and criminal matters than many clients and professionals believe.

Additionally, substance abuse counselors need to be aware that privacy guarantees for those receiving treatment for substance abuse or dependency in federally supported agencies are subject to federal regulation.

Preserving the Confidentiality of Treatment Sessions

It is the responsibility of helping professionals to ensure the confidentiality of any professional relationship, including what transpires during treatment sessions and even that such a relationship exists. This responsibility includes ensuring that:

- Counseling sessions not be recorded or observed without the client's consent
- Casework notes and discussion be limited to relevant material about the client—that is, information necessary to enhance therapeutic progress or required by funders
- All records be kept in secure places
- If the client's specific problems are used for teaching and training, the client's identity is disguised
- Envelopes containing bills for services not include the name of the treatment facility or the counselor in the return address
- When the client/counselor relationship ends, records of the relationship are disposed of after a specified amount of time, or retained in a manner that preserves the former client's privacy

Also, it is important that professionals discuss clinical information about clients only in appropriate settings. For example, hallway or elevator consultations between supervisor and counselor or among counselors can result in the accidental disclosure of confidential client information and must be avoided.

Records

Who legally and ethically "owns" client records is an important issue that has a simple answer: the client does. The simplicity of the answer, however, has complicated implications. For one thing, since the client "owns" the records, he or she has every right to see everything that is in them.

In general, all records relating to a specific counseling relationship are considered professional information for use by the specific counselor for the benefit of the specific client—they are not a part of the overall records of the organization for which the counselor works. This refers to interview notes, case notes, test results, correspondence, and other material directly related to the client. Such records should remain held on behalf of the client in the custody of the counselor and not be mingled with those of other counselors. In some states, however, regulations or procedures required by funding agencies may specify differently, and those regulations will have to be adhered to. But everyone needs to be aware that there are obvious disclosure risks—and possible ethical violations—associated with the mingling of records to which a number of people have some form of access.

Also, as more and more organizations use central computer-based data storage, there must be safeguards put in place so that unlimited access to information about a specific client is restricted to that client's counselor. While ultimately the way in which data storage is handled may be beyond the individual helping professional's ability to control, practitioners should do what they can to protect the privacy of their clients, including pointing out administrative decisions that endanger it.

Professionals and clerical staff need to be especially careful about the information they exchange on the phone, even with others they believe to be entitled to information about clients. In most cases, the fact that an individual is receiving help from a specific helping organization is itself confidential information. For this reason, responding to any sort of question over the phone about a client is dangerous and should be avoided.

Most people like to be helpful, and many breaches of confidentiality occur accidentally under the guise of help. A question from a phone caller about whether a certain individual is expected for an appointment on a certain day, for example, may seem innocent, but it could be a way of establishing client status. Those who handle phone calls should respectfully decline to answer any questions regarding clients, saying something like: "I'm sorry, but it is the policy of this agency not to answer any questions about individuals who may or may not be clients. Official inquiries should be addressed to the agency in writing. If this is an emergency, I will have my supervisor phone you if you will leave your name and number." Having the supervisor call rather than transferring the caller may help establish who the caller is and/or represents.

Faxing information is also dangerous since it is rarely clear who is at the receiving end. In general, we believe that client-identifying information should not be faxed. If it is, practitioners need to make sure that some sort of safeguards are in place to ensure that the information will go only into the hands of those who are entitled to it.

It is also not always clear who is at the sending end of a fax. It is easy to paste an official letterhead on a request for information, making the request appear to be legitimate. In two recent incidents, prisoners were released from jail as a result of phony faxes sent by friends. Most faxes automatically include information about the sending fax phone number and location at the top of the page. At the very least, this should be routinely checked against the information on the letterhead to ensure that the request is legitimate.

Uses and Limitations of Waivers and Informed Consent Statements

General Waivers

As indicated a number of times elsewhere in this book, there are circumstances under which it is helpful to both client and counselor for the counselor to share confidential client information with others, and particularly with other professionals.

When a professional believes sharing information would be helpful to a client and wishes to do so, it is the practitioner's ethical responsibility to ensure that an appropriate waiver of confidentiality rights is signed by the client and that its meaning is fully understood. When two or more professionals are involved in some sort of treatment of the same individual, all must have signed waivers before a discussion can take place.

Informed Consent Forms

"Informed consent" is another kind of waiver of confidentiality rights. Such consent from clients is needed for:

- Specific kinds of treatment that may have possible unusual or unintended consequences
- The recording, observation, or discussion of therapeutic sessions
- Use of a specific client's problems in teaching or training when doing so might reveal the client's identity

There are two purposes of such forms:

- Ensuring that the client has sufficient information about the activity and possible consequences to allow him or her the opportunity to refuse it
- Protecting the professional from possible misconduct or malpractice charges that could result from a failure to disclose such information to the client

In general, professionals need to think carefully before they ask clients to consent to activities that might compromise them or have unintended consequences. The imbalance of power between counselor and client is so marked that in many cases clients will consent to virtually anything their counselor or therapist seems to want them to do. It is the professional's responsibility to protect clients against possible negative consequences that the client may not be able to see or weigh.

Insurance Company Waivers

Many insurance companies require those they insure to sign waivers of confidentiality rights before they will approve payment for treatment. Both counselors and their clients whose treatment bills are being paid by health plans need to understand that some of these waivers give the health plan's employees unlimited access to details about the reasons for treatment, including case notes. When this is the case, the counselor should let the client know since some clients may choose to pay for treatment themselves rather than risk future disclosure.

State and Federal Laws

There are a number of state and federal laws and regulations requiring specific conduct on the part of the helping professional, and some of these laws and regulations may appear to be in conflict with professional ethical standards. All state and federal laws relating to helping professionals need to be studied carefully and discussed thoroughly with supervisors and knowledgeable associates. While detailed discussion of the legalities of confidentiality issues is beyond the scope of this book, all helping professionals need to understand at least the fundamentals of such issues.

All 50 states have extended to counselor/client relationships the same privilege extended to attorney/client relationships. This means that in state courts, counselors and therapists cannot be required to give testimony or turn over notes or records of therapy sessions. The single exception to this is when the counselor or agency is being sued by the client for malpractice. In such cases, turning over privileged information is permissible because the client has, in effect, waived his or her rights to confidentiality by bringing suit.

In this connection, it's important for therapists and counselors to understand that there is a legal difference between testimony—which is protected—and evidence—which is not. That is, if you have a crack-addicted client who leaves his crack pipe in your office, goes out and commits a crime, and is identified as a client of yours, you can't be made to discuss either his addiction or your treatment for it (testimony), but you can be made to turn over the crack pipe (evidence).

Despite this protection, though, the prudent practitioner will be cautious about what goes in written records such as case notes because there are circumstances under which this privilege can be breached. For example, as discussed below in "Qualifications on Limits of Confidentiality," this privilege may not apply when a practitioner believes that others may be endangered by client behavior.

At this writing, as a general rule, state courts recognize counselor/client relationships as privileged, whereas federal courts do not.

Qualifications on Limits of Confidentiality

Broad as it is, the ethical requirement of confidentiality is not unqualified. Such qualifications include the duty to warn and the duty to inform.

Duty to Warn

Helping professionals have both an ethical and a legal obligation to report to appropriate authorities any past or potential "clear and imminent danger" that they learn about during the course of counseling. This refers to danger to the client (for example, the threat of suicide) as well as danger to others. For the most part these requirements are in state legal codes, but federal law also requires the notification of authorities in cases of child abuse.

Additionally, following a 1976 case in California, the duty to warn rule is being extended by an increasing number of states to require counselor/therapist notification of potential victims as well as authorities.

While these legal requirements may seem to be a clear violation of the ethical requirements regarding confidentiality, they are, in fact, in the best interests of society to protect others from harm; and in cases of potential harm, society's interests override those of an individual client.

Obviously, determining when past activities or threats regarding future actions are fact or fantasy requires good instincts by counselors.

Furthermore, some of these qualifications are themselves qualified. If, for example, a counselor has a good reason to believe a client has or is about to commit a crime, in some states she must notify appropriate authorities of the situation, but not of the fact that she has the information because she is treating the individual.

Also, in many states, the duty to warn requirement is specifically suspended in instances in which a counselor learns that a client has tested positive for HIV or has AIDS. That is, since those who might have been infected by the client may be in "clear and imminent danger" of infection themselves, under other circumstances the counselor would have a duty to warn those he could identify. This duty has been suspended in many states unless formal written consent from the client has been obtained.

Note that state laws in respect to confidentiality vary and have a tendency to change rapidly in the face of what lawmakers see as "the public interest." Helping professionals need to be sure that their supervisors inform them about significant changes in the law as they take place.

Duty to Inform

Under some circumstances, helping professionals have a legal duty to break confidentiality by informing appropriate authorities when they learn of or strongly suspect certain activities. By federal law, these include child abuse, and in many states and communities elder abuse, domestic violence, and the likelihood of suicide must all be reported.

Guidelines

As a useful rule of thumb, here are the occasions in which client-identifying disclosures *must* be made by all counselors:

- During a medical emergency when information about treatment and medications is needed for the protection of the client
- When presented with a court order that specifically overrides state or federal confidentiality regulations
- When there is a "clear and imminent danger" of a client committing suicide
- In most states, when there is a "clear and imminent danger" to others
- In cases of child abuse
- In cases of a lawsuit by a client against a professional or his or her employer
- In some states and many communities, in cases of elder abuse and domestic violence

Here are the occasions in which client-identifying disclosures *may* be made:

- When a client has signed a consent form that meets legal standards
- During appropriate times within a professional's own organization, such as case review meetings with supervisors; at these reviews, all individuals in the organization who receive such information—including support staff—need to be aware of and respect confidentiality requirements

Since the risks to counselors and their organizations are high from both too much and too little disclosure, it is important that supervisors, experienced colleagues, and/or attorneys be consulted when any doubt occurs.

Substance Abuse Counselors

As indicated earlier, federal law (42 CFA Part 2) regulates disclosures about "federally assisted" individuals receiving treatment for substance abuse and those who are not directly assisted but receive treatment from organizations receiving any form of federal assistance. "Federally assisted" individuals include those who receive Medicaid or Medicare benefits, and "federally assisted" organizations include any organization that has IRS status as a tax-exempt organization, so this law is broader in its application than it might at first appear to be.

In general, this federal law puts more restrictions on client-identifying disclosures for substance abuse counselors than do either ethical requirements of other counselors or state laws. There is no "duty to warn" about possible injury to others by substance abuse clients under federal law, for example. Such a warning in these cases is allowed only in cases of possible injury to others in the counselor's agency or to agency property. However, substance abuse counselors who find themselves in what would otherwise be a "duty to warn" situation should carefully consider and weigh possible consequences of notifying both authorities and potential victims.

Again, this is very complicated—and in some cases risky—stuff. Consultation with experienced professionals is essential when in doubt.

Ethical Dilemmas for Discussion and Resolution

The authors' suggestions for resolution of these dilemmas are in Chapter 12.

1. I work for an agency that operates from several different locations so that services can be available where clients live. This works well for direct service delivery and is of clear benefit to our clients in this respect. But sometimes clients move and their records need to be handed over to another location. Also, records administration is centralized in one office, which means we're constantly sending copies of what in theory is confidential information about our clients back and forth in a variety of ways. I can see the need to do this, but in these circumstances how do I meet my own ethical responsibilities?

2. Lots of clients of the agency I work for have had trouble with the law. Many are being treated by us as a result of court referrals. In many cases, the local criminal justice system wants reports from us about progress, difficulties, our own observations, and so on. Some information they want on a set schedule; some they want quickly in response to a request. The routine updates are easily handled with procedures we've set up, but I'm not very comfortable when I have to respond to requests for information about a specific client quickly, especially by phone or fax. How can I react to these requests ethically?

3. I have a client who has been referred to me by the courts for treatment. As one of the conditions of her parole, she is required to see me at least once a week. The problem is that she really doesn't. Sometimes she'll be very faithful to our schedule; sometimes she'll disappear for a few weeks, but she always comes back. Under the agreement my agency has with the courts, her parole officer is supposed to contact me for regular updates, but he has never done so. Am I ethically required to take the initiative to tell the parole officer that my client is not really fulfilling her obligations to the court?

4. My agency has relatively stringent rules about protecting client confidentiality in terms of the transfer of records, records administration, and so on. The problem is that those of us who have to comply with these rules are carrying what most of us believe are unrealistically high caseloads. This puts me and the others here in a bind. If we do our best for our clients, we don't really have time to go by the book as far as confidentiality rules are concerned. And if we go by the book on confidentiality, we don't have time to give our clients the attention they need. How do I deal with this in an ethical way?

5. My agency keeps merging with others to increase efficiency. In the process, we seem to be growing increasingly bureaucratic, in the sense that some like myself deliver direct services to clients, and others—sometimes not even here at the agency—take care of the paperwork. Before these mergers, we service providers either did most of the paperwork ourselves or had direct contact with the people who did. I'm satisfied that my peers and I are following the ethical and legal requirements regarding confidentiality, but I have no such confidence in the work of the administrative personnel, most of whom are clerks and are treated as such. What are my ethical responsibilities here?

6. A new female client says she was sexually harassed by a former therapist. She doesn't want to press charges because she says she wants to put it behind her and is afraid of her name getting back to the former therapist. I know that I'm ethically required to report or at least confront this kind of unethical behavior on the part of a colleague, but may I do this without my client's permission? I feel I have to do something.

7. I have a client who is HIV+. He says he occasionally has unprotected sex with various

partners because he fears the rejection he might experience if he shares his status with them. What are my ethical responsibilities in cases like this?

8. I have a colleague who is always curious about some of my clients. She keeps pressing me for details about their problems and what we're working through together. She's not my supervisor so she has no reason to know any of the information she seems to want. On the other hand, she's a good friend and I'm sure she wouldn't repeat anything I told her. What should I do?

THE ETHICAL DILEMMA RESOLUTION WORKSHEET

Use this form as a guide when resolving each ethical dilemma. Doing so is a good way to ensure that all steps are taken to reach a satisfactory decision.

1. The ethical standard or principle involved

2. Ethical trap possibilities

3. Preliminary response

4. Possible consequences of adopting this response

5. Ethical resolution

CHAPTER 7

Research and Publication

The Ethical Standards

Helping professionals who conduct research projects and publish the results, or who write books and articles, must follow the conventions of scholarly inquiry and publication. The ethical behavior required includes:

- Acceptance of responsibility:

  If the effort involves more than one person, the principal researcher or author should accept responsibility to hold all parties to accepted ethical standards, which should be spelled out at the start of the project.

  All researchers using human subjects are responsible for ensuring their physical and emotional welfare during the course of the project, including follow-up interviews when appropriate.

  Researchers may not withhold treatment from individuals who need it for control or comparison purposes.

  Counselors who agree to cooperate with others in projects must abide by their agreements.

  Results of studies of scientific or professional value must be made available to other members of the profession.

  There must be an opportunity to debrief participants.

- Clients who are used in research projects must voluntarily give informed consent for their participation.
- Research results must be reported in a way that accurately reflects the results.
- The intellectual property of others—including copyrights—must be respected by all researchers and authors.

Research can play an important part in furthering the knowledge and effectiveness of the people who conduct it. When this work is published, others in their profession and society as a whole can benefit as well. For these reasons research is encouraged. But those conducting research projects need to understand the ethical requirements involved.

Responsibility

Primary responsibility for conducting a research project in strict adherence to ethical standards rests with the principal researcher. All others involved in the project have a responsibility to conduct their own activities in connection with the project in an ethical way, too. In order to meet this shared responsibility, the principal researcher needs to make clear at the start of any project what ethical standards are to be observed and must conduct periodic checks to be sure the standards are observed by all involved.

All researchers using human subjects are responsible for the subjects' welfare throughout the project. This means researchers must take all reasonable precautions to avoid emotionally or physically harming anyone who participates as a subject in the project.

In some cases, research involves comparing "control" individuals who are not receiving the treatment being researched with those who are. The welfare of the control subjects needs to be protected. Researchers must carefully think through the ethical implications of withholding treatment from some selected individuals simply in order to validate research assumptions. Should the withheld treatment actually be needed, withholding it for such purposes would be unethical.

Professionals who agree to cooperate with others in research projects have the responsibility to follow through on their agreements. In doing so, they need to meet deadlines set by the principal researcher and, of course, to make sure that the information they supply is accurate and complete. Before agreeing to participate, researchers need to be sure they have the time to accomplish their part of the project.

Researchers who complete studies that are of professional or scientific value have the ethical responsibility to make the results known to other members of their profession. This is the case even when the results reflect unfavorably on institutions, programs, or services in which the researcher has an interest.

Informed Consent

Participation in a research project must be voluntary on the part of a client or other subject. All implications of the project and participation—especially potential risks, if any—must be spelled out and formal consent based on this information must be secured from each participant before the project begins. Besides being informed fully and truthfully of the study's purpose and potential risks, participants should be informed about the possibility that they may be needed later for debriefing about the project.

In some rare cases, client knowledge about the purpose of the project may influence the results. When this is the case, this ethical rule may be waived, but only when it is absolutely clear that uninformed participation will have no harmful effects on the client and is essential to the research being conducted.

The requirement for informed consent may not be waived in those cases in which subjects will be at risk in any way.

It's probably obvious but still needs to be said that in reporting research results or making original data available to other researchers, the identity of clients or other subjects must be disguised unless specific authorization to reveal this information has been secured from the client.

Reporting Results

Extreme care must be taken by researchers to report the results of their investigations in a way that accurately reflects the results and minimizes the possibility that the results will be misleading or misinterpreted.

Besides requiring clear and unambiguous writing, careful editing, and objective peer review, this also means that research reports need to be very specific about variables and conditions that might influence the data or its interpretation. Studies in which the subjects are all (or mostly) white males, for example, may not be valid for either women or minority males. Descriptions of the study and commentary about its findings should include specific information about the population studied.

Researchers who publish reports are ethically obligated to make available to qualified interested parties who may want to replicate their studies enough original research data or other information for them to do so. This includes a requirement to make human subjects who have participated in the research available for debriefing or other forms of interviewing to establish validity.

It is important that researchers take the time to become familiar with previous work in the area they are studying and give recognition to it when appropriate. It is especially important to become familiar with and observe all copyright laws.

Beyond that, authors of research papers should give due credit by means of joint authorship, acknowledgments, footnote statements, or in other ways to those who have contributed significantly to the research or the writing of the report.

Intellectual Property

A great deal of what helping professionals know they learn in classes, seminars, and workshops given by other professionals in their own or related fields and from reading the work of others. Over a period of time, it is sometimes difficult to distinguish between original ideas and those received from others. It is important, though, when writing on a professional subject, to identify carefully the sources of information used and to give credit to those whose ideas have been expanded upon and to acknowledge all who have influenced the present work. This same ethical principle holds when lecturing or giving workshops.

Ethical Dilemmas for Discussion and Resolution

The authors' suggestions for resolution of these dilemmas are in Chapter 12.

1. I agreed to help a colleague with a book she's working on by drafting two or three chapters relating to my specialty. The problem is that I have now been offered a project that would pay more, but only if I complete it very quickly. The two projects have about the same deadline dates and I can't do both. If I tell my colleague that I can't write the chapters now, she could probably find someone else. Don't you think that would be all right?

2. I've been working on a complicated research project trying to quantify the results of a certain kind of treatment. We are using questionnaires about current behavior. As I see it, one problem we have here is that our study population is highly diverse and those of us

who are conducting the study are not. The questionnaire seems straightforward enough to us, but I'm not really sure how some of the subjects will interpret the questions. If they interpret them differently than we intended, the results will be affected in one way or another. What do you suggest to make this an ethically acceptable study?

3. I want to conduct a research project using as subjects the members of several groups I facilitate. Members of the groups seem to like me and want to be helpful, so I'm sure they'll cooperate. But this tendency to be helpful can have a downside because if I tell them exactly what I'm trying to find out, I'm sure they'll either know or try to guess how I want them to respond and act accordingly, rather than telling me what they really believe. I know that ethically I'm supposed to give them all this information, but I'm sure that if I do so the results might not have much validity. What should I do?

4. Someone I know has some interesting theories about the field we both work in and has been writing a book about them. While she certainly has the experience and expertise to write about the subject, she doesn't have the academic background. A prospective publisher has told her he is interested in the book, but only if she can get someone with better academic credentials as a co-author to give it acceptability, believing that her lack of advanced degrees will stand in the way of the book's acceptance. I have the advanced degrees she lacks, and she has asked if I would agree to become the co-author. While I think I agree with her theories in general, she's on a tight deadline schedule that doesn't allow me enough time to review the material completely, let alone actually contribute to it. Is it ethical to be listed as the co-author?

THE ETHICAL DILEMMA RESOLUTION WORKSHEET

Use this form as a guide when resolving each ethical dilemma. Doing so is a good way to ensure that all steps are taken to reach a satisfactory decision.

1. The ethical standard or principle involved

2. Ethical trap possibilities

3. Preliminary response

4. Possible consequences of adopting this response

5. Ethical resolution

CHAPTER 8

Measurement, Evaluation, and Testing

The Ethical Standards

Helping professionals who use qualitative or quantitative tests to evaluate or assess clients or groups of clients must do so in a manner that ensures validity and confidentiality of results. Ethical requirements include:

- Ensuring that each test used is:

  Appropriate for the purpose for which it is being used

  Likely to produce valid results for the individual or group to whom it is given

  Statistically reliable in what it finds

- Disclosing to the client or clients taking the test its purpose so that participation is voluntary
- Administering tests under the conditions for which they were designed
- Scoring and interpreting test results in strict accordance with test instructions
- Administering tests only by professionals who are competent to do so
- Ensuring adequate security for test questions so that they are not known in advance when this is necessary to produce valid results
- Adhering to copyright restrictions

Helping professionals in many fields use tests and other measuring devices to evaluate or appraise individual clients or groups of clients in an objective way. The following ethical requirements pertain to the administration and interpretation of any of these tests.

Reliability, Validity, and Appropriateness

Standardized tests have specific uses and limitations. Professionals using these tests must understand what the uses and limitations are and select the tests and measuring devices they use carefully. There are two requirements each test should meet:

1. That it is appropriate and reliable as a measurement of whatever the tester is trying to measure
2. That results are likely to be valid for the individual or group taking the test

While these requirements should be met by any test, they are especially important for tests used for vocational or educational selection, placement, or to determine the need for counseling or therapy. Tests for these purposes that cannot withstand scrutiny on the basis of their validity, reliability, or appropriateness in specific cases may be challenged on legal as well as ethical grounds.

Those who give tests also need to recognize that clients can become test-wise. In general, the more times the same test is given to a client, the less likely it is to produce valid results. Professionals who use tests to track changes in clients' status should be careful about using the same test routinely and choose alternative tests from time to time.

Disclosure of Purpose

There are two ethical issues here.

One is the issue of choice. Those administering tests have an ethical obligation to inform those taking them what the purpose of the test is so the test-takers may make an informed decision about whether or not they want to participate.

The other is that tests given to those who do not understand their purpose or the specific way in which they should be completed are likely to produce invalid or misleading results. Thus:

- Those being tested need to be fully informed about how the results will be used before the test is given.
- Potential test-takers should have the opportunity to refuse to take a test after they know its purpose.
- Test instructions must be followed carefully to ensure that the answers given result in compatible or interpretable data.

Testing Conditions

Different tests are designed to be administered under different circumstances and conditions. Those giving tests need to make sure they understand the conditions under which the tests they are administering are likely to produce valid results and when they won't.

For example, there are tests that establish general personal interests or opinions, and these are appropriately administered by mail or without qualified supervision. But tests that measure knowledge or understanding must be administered under close supervision by trained, objective, and responsible individuals. It is unethical to administer tests under conditions other than those for which they were designed.

Additionally, those administering and supervising test-taking need to be aware of and note any unusual circumstances or behavior that occur during the testing session and take them into consideration when scoring the test. If, for example, during a testing session a member of the group taking the test is disruptive or unruly, test results could be influenced and need to be evaluated in this context.

Scoring and Interpretation

Test results must be scored in strict compliance with test instructions in order to produce meaningful results.

Interpretation of test results to clients and others who are not familiar with their limitations must be provided very carefully to avoid misconceptions and misinterpretations. Helping professionals need to be sensitive to the fact that certain terms related to test results, such as IQ, grade equivalent scores, percentiles, and standard deviations, are loaded and easy to misinterpret by people who do not fully understand them.

Those using the results of tests also need to understand that the norms and standards for some tests are based on the accumulated results from certain specific groups or populations. It is especially important to be cautious when evaluating and interpreting the test performance of minority group members (socioeconomic, ethnic, or cultural) who may not have been included in the norms for which the test is standard.

On the other hand, test evaluators need to be equally cautious about manipulating test scores to adjust for these differences. Unvalidated information about "typical" differences from the norms may be used for a specific test, but only very carefully. Such manipulation must be revealed as part of the test results.

Competence

Not all helping professionals are competent by experience and training to administer all tests. It must be recognized that different tests require different levels of competence, and professionals should administer, score, and interpret only those tests for which they are actually qualified to do so. Major sources of standardized tests specify levels of training and experience needed to administer each test they supply. These requirements should be followed by test administrators.

At the same time, not all tests can produce meaningful results for all people. The most obvious example is a written test given to someone who is illiterate. Tests in English given to Spanish-speakers is another. And cultural differences need to be considered whenever tests are given to culturally diverse test-takers so that the results are meaningful.

Security

The results of many tests are meaningless if the person taking them knows the questions or answers in advance. It is the test administrator's responsibility to ensure that there is no coaching or prior distribution of or access to test questions.

Violation of Copyrights

Most standardized tests are copyrighted by those who design them. Tempting as it may be, it's unethical to either duplicate or modify these tests without the prior approval of the copyright owner.

Ethical Dilemmas for Discussion and Resolution

The authors' suggestions for resolution of these dilemmas are in Chapter 12.

1. I understand that I am supposed to tell my clients how their test results will be used. I work with alcohol and other drug addicts referred by the courts. If I tell them I'm going to

use the test results as part of my diagnosis and recommendations, they'll lie on the test. What should I do?

2. My client says he is having a hard time concentrating when trying to complete a standardized personality test in my office. He wants to take the test home and complete it there. I want him to feel comfortable, but I am concerned about the ethical implications if I grant his request.

3. I am a human services worker in a mental health treatment facility. One of my clients has asked for the opportunity to learn more about his own issues through psychological testing. I do think he could benefit from the focus that testing can provide. I took a course on tests and measurements while working on my associate's degree. Can I go ahead and administer the tests?

4. After taking a battery of tests as part of an employment application for the county mental health board, I was given the test data to look over and review. I really didn't know what I was looking at, and it kind of bothered me to see that on certain test results my scores were in the 60th percentile. Does this mean I flunked the test? How can I make sense of this?

5. My agency insists that we use certain pen-and-paper assessment tools with our clients. The results are used to validate a client's diagnosis and subsequent treatment plan. I am convinced that not all of my clients truly understand the questions. Not everyone I work with can read at the same level, and some are actually illiterate. I've considered altering the language of the test to make it more readable. How can I comply with my agency's requirements and guarantee fair and accurate test results for my clients?

THE ETHICAL DILEMMA RESOLUTION WORKSHEET

Use this form as a guide when resolving each ethical dilemma. Doing so is a good way to ensure that all steps are taken to reach a satisfactory decision.

1. The ethical standard or principle involved

2. Ethical trap possibilities

3. Preliminary response

4. Possible consequences of adopting this response

5. Ethical resolution

CHAPTER 9

Teaching and Training

The Ethical Standards

- Teachers and trainers must offer instruction only in areas in which they have professional expertise.
- While final authority in such matters rests with appropriate credentialing organizations, teachers and trainers should use their formal evaluations to encourage professional advancement only to those who are competent.

Professional Expertise

Some who are certified as helping professionals both provide direct services to clients and teach and train others as well. Those who do so have an ethical responsibility to offer instruction only in those areas of study in which they have actual academic and/or practical experience in sufficient depth to teach others about it. Simply having read the text or having the ability to keep one step ahead of learners is not ethically sufficient. Additionally, those who teach have an ethical responsibility to develop the ability to present material in a way that is understandable to learners and that encourages them to learn.

Responsibility to the Public and the Profession

The Public

All helping professionals have an ethical obligation to use their experience and expertise to inform the public about problems and opportunities affecting their professional specialty and their client populations. This is important to gain public support for their work and understanding of their clients and their special needs.

Those who wish to take public positions on issues relating to their profession are encouraged to do so. However, many organizations restrict the number of individuals who can actually speak for the organization. When this is the case and the professional is not an officially designated spokesperson but still wants to make her opinions known, it is the professional's responsibility to make it clear that she is speaking as an individual and not as a representative of the organization. Additionally, if a professional finds he disagrees with his organization on a specific point and still wants to speak out, it would be wise for him to consult with his supervisor before doing so.

The Profession

Those who teach others who would like to become helping professionals have an ethical responsibility to the public and to their profession to use their position as advisors to encourage those they believe are likely to become good practitioners and discourage those who are not, recognizing that final determination in such matters is generally the responsibility of credentialing organizations.

This does not, of course, suggest that subjective opinions on the part of teachers or trainers about the future overall competence or suitability of individual learners should lead them to withhold good grades or evaluations in specific subjects.

Ethical Dilemmas for Discussion and Resolution

The authors' suggestions for resolution of these dilemmas are in Chapter 12.

1. I am offering a course on counseling alcohol and other drug dependent people. Although I have had no formal professional training or experience, I have learned a great deal through my own personal experiences. I am in recovery from alcohol and other drug addictions myself and have successfully worked with others. A local counselor has questioned the ethics of my teaching such a class without "proper credentials." Aren't my years of personal experience enough?
2. I have been training human services professionals for a number of years now. Recently I met with a colleague and compared training evaluation results. His were consistently better than mine. I always assumed my low evaluations were due to the lack of responsiveness of my burned-out student workers rather than my abilities as a teacher. Do I have some kind of ethical problem here?
3. I am putting together a course for my agency co-workers on dealing with clients referred by the criminal justice system. All the materials I have are from my academic and professional training nearly 15 years ago. Some of the newer workers are questioning my expertise. I don't see why my material is not still valid. I can't believe things have changed all that much. What should I do?

THE ETHICAL DILEMMA RESOLUTION WORKSHEET

Use this form as a guide when resolving each ethical dilemma. Doing so is a good way to ensure that all steps are taken to reach a satisfactory decision.

1. The ethical standard or principle involved

2. Ethical trap possibilities

3. Preliminary response

4. Possible consequences of adopting this response

5. Ethical resolution

CHAPTER 10

Consulting and Private Practice

The Ethical Standards

Helping professionals in private practice are required to adhere to the ethical standards of their own specialty. In addition, there are a number of ethical requirements that pertain particularly to those who practice privately. For example:

- Professionals who act as consultants to organizations must:

    Do so only within their own areas of expertise.

    Set clearly defined goals with which to evaluate effectiveness.

    Ensure that such relationships are of limited duration to foster client self-dependence.

- Professionals who are employed by an organization may not charge a private fee to a client who is entitled to the services from the professional's employer.
- Professionals who both work for an organization and see clients privately, or who work for more than one employer, must recognize possible limitations to their own professional effectiveness that might result from becoming overextended.
- Professionals in private practice must not overstate their qualifications or give inappropriate outcome assurances when marketing their services.
- Professionals in group private practice must work to maintain the highest ethical standards within the group.

Many helping professionals are in private practice either alone or as members of a group. Many others even though employed by agencies augment their incomes by seeing clients on their own time unless their employer has a prohibition against doing so. And still others work under contract with more than one employer. In all these cases, they will guide their behavior by the general ethical standards of their profession, but there are also specific ethical requirements that they need to be aware of. We consider these requirements below.

Fees

It is unethical for a professional to accept a private fee from clients who are entitled to these services from the professional's employer. In many cases, agencies will have a policy about who may and who may not be seen privately by professionals in their employ. In those cases, these policies should be scrupulously followed.

It is both unethical and illegal to waive co-payment fees when they are required by third-party funders such as insurance companies. If an insurance company paying a part of your client's fees for your services requires that a sum of money also be paid by the client to you, you must insist that this actually happens.

Finally on this subject, it is unethical to change fees during the course of treatment unless it has been made clear at the outset of treatment that fees may be raised at some point and the client.is given notice well before an impending change. Clients need certainty in their lives, especially financial certainty.

Private practitioners in single or group practice who control their own fee structures should carefully note the ethical requirement for nondiscrimination on financial grounds and abide by it. Some private practitioners earmark a percentage of their time for no- or low-pay clients. Many have a sliding fee scale based on clients' relative abilities to pay. Others, faced with potential clients who do not have the ability to pay their normal fees, simply refer them to practitioners or agencies that can provide good treatment at lower cost. The major issue here is to ensure that proper treatment is given or services provided to all who need them.

Professional Effectiveness

Employed professionals should acknowledge that their first responsibility is to their employer (and clients) in terms of giving full time and attention to the position they hold. It is important for practitioners who see clients outside their agencies to remember that everyone has energy and attention limitations. When these are exceeded, the quality of their work and their usefulness to their clients suffer. Professionals who take on outside clients when they are fully engaged with their employer's clients are in danger of acting unethically in terms of both their employer and their clients.

In this connection, it's also important to remember the need everyone has to live fully rounded lives. Helping professionals who neglect their own lives in order to see additional outside clients or log extra hours at work need to examine their priorities and values.

Finally, professionals need to be careful about how they define their "own time" as opposed to that of their employer's. That is, while they may certainly use vacation or compensatory time to see outside clients, they should not use sick time for this purpose.

Consulting

Helping professionals who act as consultants to organizations or individuals have an ethical responsibility to make sure they do not overestimate or overstate their qualifications for doing so. They also need to make sure that both they and their clients have clearly defined and understood goals so that judgments about successful consultation can be made against objective and mutually agreed-upon criteria.

When acting as consultants, professionals need to set clear time limits for the relationship. This means that one of their goals should be client self-direction, and they should not act in a way that encourages future dependency on them as a consultant.

Private Practice

Specific ethical codes for professionals in private practice involve the conditions under which they may advertise or otherwise market their services. The major ethical concern is that private practitioners not overstate their qualifications and/or give inappropriate outcome assurances to prospective clients.

In general, private practitioners should limit their marketing claims to an accurate recital of their highest relevant degrees, level of certification or license, the type and description of services offered, and other similar objective information. Claims about therapeutic results need to be made very carefully, if at all. In this and other respects, private practitioners should be aware of and adhere to local regulations regarding the advertising of counseling services.

Group Practice

Each professional in group practice with other professionals has an obligation to maintain the highest ethical standards for the practice as a whole. If a professional discovers what may be unethical behavior on the part of another professional in the practice, the following sequence of events should be used:

1. Informally confront in an effort to resolve the issue privately.
2. If this is unsuccessful, report concerns to the appropriate credentialing authority.
3. Resign if a lack of resolution reflects on your professional competence or the welfare of group members.

Ethical Dilemmas for Discussion and Resolution

The authors' suggestions for resolution of these dilemmas are in Chapter 12.

1. I have completed my bachelor's degree in a human services field. All of my professors praised my ability to interact well with my internship clients. I feel confident that I am qualified to counsel others and believe that I can be of help to many. As a result, I have opened up my own practice as a psychotherapist. I have been careful not to use terms in my advertising that imply that I have a specific license. I do, however, list myself as a psychotherapist, which is not a legal term. At a professional meeting, a local social worker challenged the ethics of my advertising. Could she be right?
2. I am a provider of mental health services for a local insurance company. The insurance company reimburses 80% of my normal hourly fee. Some of my clients have a difficult time paying even their 20% co-payment. In some cases I have agreed to treat them for the 80% insurance reimbursement, waiving their co-pay. I read an article recently that implies that this is insurance fraud and is considered unethical as well. What should I do?
3. The mental health board in my area has asked me to consult with its staff in regard to the treatment of alcohol and other drug dependent clients. These clients have mental illnesses of some sort and are drug abusers as well. I have a great deal of experience in the area of counseling drug abusers but none in the area of mental illnesses. Plus I've never been a consultant before. Am I truly qualified?

4. I work as a private practitioner in a group assessment and counseling service. I suspect that one of my colleagues is engaging in dual relationships with his clients. Quite honestly, I don't know if this is really any of my business. Besides, if I confront him, there might be repercussions such as a decrease in my referrals from him. On the other hand, if I'm right about his unethical behavior and it becomes public knowledge, the whole practice could be damaged. What should I do?

THE ETHICAL DILEMMA RESOLUTION WORKSHEET

Use this form as a guide when resolving each ethical dilemma. Doing so is a good way to ensure that all steps are taken to reach a satisfactory decision.

1. The ethical standard or principle involved

2. Ethical trap possibilities

3. Preliminary response

4. Possible consequences of adopting this response

5. Ethical resolution

CHAPTER 11

Ethics for Supervisors

Although most users of this manual are students and professionals in training, the realities of the helping professions are such that people are often moved very quickly into supervisory positions. One purpose here is to help those who become supervisors to understand the specific ethical responsibilities they will have in that position.

Additionally, it is useful for those new to the field to understand what they have a right to expect from those who supervise their work.

The Ethical Standards

- Supervisors have a responsibility to create and maintain an ethical workplace for those they supervise and their clients.
- Supervisors need to be aware that they have responsibility for ensuring the ethical behavior of their trainees and that they share responsibility for any ethical violations of those they supervise.
- Supervisors should ensure that support staff understand and adhere to the ethical standards of the agency for which they work.
- Supervisors should report violations of ethical standards to appropriate authorities when necessary.
- Supervisors should provide those they supervise with formal goals, reviews, and feedback and the opportunity for professional advancement.
- Supervisors need to make sure that they have sufficient opportunity for professional development and feedback.

Creating and Maintaining an Ethical Workplace

Those who supervise other professionals and learners have a critical role—arguably the most critical role—in ensuring adherence to the ethical standards of their profession by those they supervise. This is because the supervisor consciously or unconsciously sets the ethical norm that guides the behavior of all those whose work they oversee and, especially, evaluate.

Supervisors who make it clear that professional ethical considerations are important and expected in all professional relationships, and reward those who apply them, will find this clarity reflected in staff behavior. On the other hand, supervisors who do not make this clear, or who are perceived to practice or condone unethical behavior, will find this lack of ethics reflected in staff behavior.

To best ensure an ethical workplace, explicit and implicit organizational standards should be set by:

- Supervisors' careful adherence to all professional ethical standards and insistence that these standards be adhered to by others as well
- Supervisors' making sure that all those under their supervision are familiar with the ethical standards of their discipline
- Supervisors' creating and maintaining a working environment that ensures co-workers the safety they need for open and honest discussion of important issues
- Supervisors' supplying copies of relevant ethical codes to those under their supervision, or making sure all personnel know where copies can be quickly found
- Supervisors' holding periodic in-house workshops on professional ethics in general and on the specific ethical issues that have or are likely to arise in the particular settings in which the professionals are working
- Supervisors' encouraging all staff members to attend professional workshops on ethics, or on specific ethical issues
- Supervisors' encouraging the discussion of ethical issues during staff meetings in a constructive and nonadversarial way
- Supervisors' carefully monitoring staff activities and behaviors to spot staff who might have ethical problems, working with them in an effort to head off future problems, or terminating the professional relationship if future problems seem likely

It is particularly important that supervisors avoid dual relationships with those they supervise. Nothing can destroy an ethical workplace faster than news of a dual relationship—especially a sexual relationship—between a supervisor and a staff member.

Liability

Apart from the general need to establish and preserve a workplace that benefits both clients and staff by functioning in an ethical manner, the steps indicated above are good protective moves for both supervisors and agency managers. The reason is that except in the case of a solo practitioner, any legal action that might result from an ethical breach on the part of anyone in an agency will almost always include both the supervisor and agency management as defendants. An affirmative policy about maintaining ethical standards backed up by training and other behavior indicating that this policy is taken seriously is the best protective defense.

Support Staff

Managed care, economic considerations, and other forces working in the helping professions as well as in medical fields are leading to the mergers of organizations and private practices into units of increasing size. While this may be fostering efficiency, it is also creating possible ethical problems that were more easily addressed in smaller offices.

For example, there is increasing use of support staff to do routine work, freeing up professionals to spend more time delivering services. But, since much of this routine work is essentially clerical in nature, there is sometimes a tendency to see it and those who do it as "nonprofessional." Yet the opportunity for support staff violations of a number of professional ethical standards is substantial, particularly with regard to confidentiality and client privacy rights. And since such violations can have serious consequences, the opportunities for them to occur should be minimized.

All support staff should be seen as professionals at what they do, regardless of job, credentials, or title, and be made familiar with and held to those professional ethical standards that apply to them. In this regard, the material in Chapter 6, "Confidentiality," regarding disclosure of information about individuals receiving treatment and in some cases the nature of treatment offered in a specific facility is especially important. Additionally, in a desire all of us have to be helpful to others, support staff individuals are sometimes more willing than they should be to offer information over the phone to persons they don't know or to fax confidential information to persons who may not be entitled to it.

A major point of ethical standards is protection, which is the responsibility of all who work in a professional setting, not just those who are licensed or credentialed. It is the responsibility of supervisors to ensure that this protection is given by all associated with an organization.

Reporting Violations

One of the most perplexing ethical problems for supervisors is when to report an ethical violation by someone under their supervision. While each such question must be answered on its own merits, here are some thoughts that supervisors might use as a decision-making guide:

- Problem avoidance is always preferable to problem remediation. Taking the steps indicated earlier to foster an ethical workplace and to weed out those who are likely to present the agency with ethical problems is the best way to avoid serious ethical issues that could threaten the organization.
- Helping professionals have a right to expect a workplace environment in which they may safely explore personal and ethical concerns with their supervisors in a non-adversarial way. Where this environment exists, potential ethical problems can often be identified and headed off before they occur.
- Supervisors have an obligation to do all they can to ensure client welfare by carefully observing the ethical practices of those they supervise and correcting tendencies they observe before violations can occur.
- Supervisors should try to resolve ethical conflicts or unethical practices within their own organizations whenever possible before reporting them to credentialing agencies.
- When this kind of informal resolution is not possible—including when serious violations have already occurred—violations should be reported. It must be kept in mind, however, that the protection of client confidentiality must be an important consideration in doing so. Thus, even when a practitioner has clearly violated an ethical code with respect to an individual client, reporting such a violation to credentialing authorities can include client-identifying information only when the client agrees to this specific disclosure.
- Supervisors need to recognize that ethical violations by those on their staffs can do serious injury to the agencies for which they work as well as to those directly involved.

This means that all aspects of an ethical violation need to be examined carefully and priorities set before it is resolved. This does not mean that ethical violations by staff members should be hidden in an effort to protect the agency. It does mean that should disclosure be necessary, it should be made in a way that protects the agency's ability to continue to function on behalf of all its clients.

- No such report should be made without consultation with other senior supervisors, experienced and respected peers, and, in some cases, knowledgeable attorneys.

Staff Career Development

Performance Goals, Reviews, and Feedback

Ethical codes that address this subject hold that both practitioners and supervisors have a responsibility to establish working relationships that are based on a clear mutual understanding of agency and individual goals and accountability for meeting them. As a practical matter, it is the supervisor's responsibility to take leadership in this, working with those she or he supervises to develop formal performance goals that are both realistic and challenging. Supervisors need to develop both formal periodic reviews of performance matched against goals and an informal process for more frequent feedback.

There are two practical reasons for this.

One is that everyone works most effectively in organizations that spell out as clearly as possible what is expected of both the organization as a whole and individual members of it. Since all organizations get the performance they reward, those who head them need to make it very clear what kind of performance they want, then make sure the performance is recognized and rewarded. This can be done only with a formal process of goal-setting, performance reviews, wage increases, and other forms of advancement tied to objective measurements.

The other is that one of the most difficult tasks of most supervisors is letting someone go because of lack of performance. While this is in any case emotionally difficult, having objective reasons for doing so (which may or may not be shared with the individual being let go) can make it somewhat easier. Additionally, mutually agreed-upon performance standards and honest reviews of both those who meet the performance standards and those who don't are the best defenses against wrongful discharge suits in an increasingly litigious society.

Education and Training

Contemporary business theory is that after ensuring effectiveness in her or his unit, it is every manager's primary responsibility to develop the professional knowledge and skills of the people supervised. This is good theory and practice in the helping professions as well.

Since all professionals have an ethical responsibility to ensure that they enhance their professional competence by keeping current with new developments in their fields, supervisors have an additional ethical responsibility to ensure that those they supervise are given every reasonable opportunity to do so.

Although this may be beyond the control of the direct supervisor, all organizations for which helping professionals work should have policies that at least encourage staff participation in courses and workshops that increase skills and learning for all professionals and for other staff members as well. Many organizations also have a policy of financially rewarding professionals for such achievements as earning advanced degrees or steps up in credentialing hierarchies. Those who do earn this kind of professional recognition should be formally recognized for this both because of their own achievements and as encouragement to others.

Self-Development and Feedback

Supervisors have the same ethical responsibility as those they supervise to enhance their own knowledge and skills and to maintain professional relationships that can provide them with honest feedback and reality checks.

They need to work to make sure that they as well as their staffs have class and workshop opportunities to enhance their clinical and administrative skills.

Feedback and reality checks may be problematic. In some ways, supervisors are in awkward positions in many organizations. Their role as performance evaluators tends to isolate them from the individuals they supervise. Then, since their own performance is evaluated by those above them in the organizational hierarchy, they can feel isolated from "top management" as well. And since in some cases supervisors are competitive with other supervisors in their own organizations for advancement, safe relationships with their peers are also sometimes difficult to build.

Supervisors who find themselves in this position should try to develop independent peer relationships with professionals they respect in other organizations to provide them with insights and feedback. Local professional organizations, classes, and workshops are good places in which to find such peers.

Ethical Dilemmas for Discussion and Resolution

The authors' suggestions for resolution of these dilemmas are in Chapter 12.

1. I am a trainee in a local social service agency. I am supposed to have weekly meetings with my supervisor. In the last two months, my supervisor has canceled six of our scheduled meetings. I am working with clients and have ensured them that I have supervision. I feel like a liar. What should I do? I don't want to make waves at this place, but I also want to do what's right.
2. One of the people I supervise is experiencing significant personal problems. These personal problems are beginning to affect his work performance. He is aware of this and has brought it up in several of our supervisory meetings. There is a great deal of trust in our relationship, and I would like to provide assistance in dealing with the problems. Would it hurt if I provide a little counseling during supervision?
3. I want the people I supervise to feel safe in our relationship to the point where they can disclose even unethical behavior if they need to so that we can resolve the problem in the best possible way. On the other hand, I don't want to be in a position to report that behavior to the credentialing board. I feel really stuck. What's a good approach?

THE ETHICAL DILEMMA RESOLUTION WORKSHEET

Use this form as a guide when resolving each ethical dilemma. Doing so is a good way to ensure that all steps are taken to reach a satisfactory decision.

1. The ethical standard or principle involved

2. Ethical trap possibilities

3. Preliminary response

4. Possible consequences of adopting this response

5. Ethical resolution

CHAPTER 12

Suggested Resolutions of Ethical Dilemmas

The resolutions suggested here are primarily for discussion purposes and were developed by following the ethical decision-making process outlined and discussed in Chapter 3.

While these resolutions represent the authors' best thinking on these issues, students and other readers should think about the information presented in each dilemma, the ethical standards involved, and reach their own conclusions.

Personal Responsibilities

Dilemma 1

Problem identification: I am a social worker employed by a county social service agency. I'm clean and sober during the week, but on weekends, we (the man I live with and some of our friends) sometimes drink pretty heavily and do drugs on occasion. Once or twice things have gotten out of hand and the police have been called. Nothing came of this, but I'm beginning to get worried about what might happen to my job if I get picked up for being under the influence or in possession of a proscribed substance. Is this an ethical issue? It does not affect my performance in any way.

PROCESS AND SUGGESTED RESPONSE

Ethical standard involved: The ethical standard involved (personal conduct) says that helping professionals should "maintain high standards of personal conduct, recognizing that while helping professionals have the same rights as other individuals in terms of personal behavior, they should not conduct themselves privately in such a way that might jeopardize their ability to function professionally."

Ethical trap possibilities: A "circumstantiality" trap may have been avoided by raising the issue.

Preliminary response: There are really two ethical problems here, one regarding abuse of alcohol, the other regarding use of what are presumably illegal drugs. Either or both could lead to arrest, which could result in sanctions from your employer, including the possible loss of employment. Any such sanction would "jeopardize your ability to function professionally," and activities that might lead to this are unethical, including those described in the dilemma. Thus, both abuse of alcohol and use of illegal drugs should stop.

Circumstantiality: The statement that the indicated behavior "does not affect my performance in any way" is not a circumstantiality consideration for a number of reasons. The most important is the unexpressed end of it—"at this time." Alcohol and drug abuse are progressive, and professional impairment in early stages is not always easy to spot, especially by the person impaired.

Possible consequences: Apart from personal lifestyle changes for you and your partner, there are no negative short- or long-term professional consequences to your clients, yourself or your agency involved in a decision to act as the ethical standard suggests.

Ethical resolution: Cease the activities indicated in the dilemma.

Dilemma 2

Problem identification: I work for a social service agency that seems constantly to be chasing dollars. That is, it looks to me as though when the people who run the place find out about the possibility of a grant for offering a specific kind of treatment, they claim to have people on staff who are qualified to do the work, but they actually don't. Then when they get the grant, they run around trying to hire the people they claimed to have, or try to make those of us who have different kinds of training offer the treatment they're being paid to deliver. I'm sure this is an ethical violation on their part. Is it? What should I do about it?

PROCESS AND SUGGESTED RESPONSE

Ethical standard involved: There are two ethical standards regarding professional competence involved here. One says that helping professionals "should not . . . practice in specialties in which they have little or no training or professional experience." The other says that, "Besides holding themselves to this ethical standard, ethical codes require that helping professionals insist that others in their field do so, too."

Possible legal issue: While there do not seem to be any legal issues here in which you are personally involved, there may be some for your agency. That is, most grant applications require the agency or individual seeking the grant to affirm that all statements in it are true. Should your agency actually claim to have expertise it does not have, affirming that it does have them could be an illegal act that, if discovered, could have serious consequences for the agency.

Ethical trap possibilities: There is a danger of falling into the "who will benefit" trap.

Preliminary response: First of all, you should personally refrain from practicing specialties in which you have little or no training or professional experience. If you are asked to do so, you should refuse, mentioning your ethical concerns. Additionally, you should discuss your concerns about your agency's behavior with your supervisor. It may be that the agency knows about the availability in the community of professionals who can provide appropriate treatment should the grant applications be approved. If, however, as you suggest in your dilemma, the agency is simply chasing grants and attempting to retrofit existing staff to perform the work, you should consider pursuing the issue, first higher up in the agency. If this is unsuccessful, you should consider reporting the agency to credentialing or licensing authorities and resigning your position.

Circumstantiality: As stated, there are no circumstantiality issues involved in your own behavior. From the point of view of your agency, it may be that assertions about the availability of such expertise are effectively true because of the ready availability in the community of trained persons to provide the service. It may also be claimed that receiving the grant is necessary in order for the agency to grow or even function. The first of these should be considered in your response. The second should not.

Possible consequences: There are a number of possible short- and long-term professional consequences of turning this preliminary response into a more formal resolution of this dilemma. For example:

There are consequences for yourself if you either refuse to provide services you are untrained in or actually do so in violation of the code. Should you refuse to provide such services, your career at this agency could be limited. Should you do so, you violate your ethical code.

If you are currently seeing clients at this agency, their interests need to be considered, too. If you leave the agency either voluntarily or involuntarily on this issue, what will happen to their treatment? (Possible "Who will benefit" trap.)

Insisting that your agency refrain from practices that may be unethical but lead to increased revenue might be financially crippling to your agency. This consequence, plus again possible consequences for other clients, should be considered. (Possible "circumstantiality" trap.)

Will your community be harmed by the continuation of a situation in which inadequate treatment is given?

Ethical resolution: We do not find any of the possible consequences sufficiently important to change our preliminary response for the following reasons:

- Providing treatment for which you have neither training nor experience is ethically unacceptable because of possible injury to clients.
- The possible ethical trap is putting the short-term interests of your current clients ahead of long-term interests of future clients and of society, as indicated below. If you were switched to another specialty, presumably your current clients would be reassigned anyway. And if you decide to leave the agency, you can do so in a way that protects your clients.
- Making ethical decisions, either personally or organizationally, on the basis of financial considerations is a significant ethical trap and one of the most frequent reasons for ethical violations. If your agency can perform its function only in an unethical manner, it should go out of business.
- Should a funding authority find out that the agency is falsifying its claims about its treatment ability, it is highly likely that funding will be withdrawn. Other consequences of increasing severity could also be experienced.
- The community at large *is* deprived of needed services when they are claimed but not delivered. If the community in one way or another is the funder, it is also cheated of its money.

Because there are so many considerations involved in resolving an issue of this kind it is a good example of one in which objective feedback is especially important. Ultimately, however, we believe the preliminary response is the best resolution.

Dilemma 3

Problem identification: I am a substance abuse counselor, and most of my clients are women who have substance abuse problems to a varying degree. I know all of the warning signs of drug dependence, and I'm pretty well free of them myself, but there are times when things get too much for me and I go off and get drunk, usually by myself. This doesn't happen often, but it does happen often enough so that I'm aware of it. Sometimes when I'm discussing with a client her use of drugs, I find myself downplaying my feelings about how much she's using because it seems to match my own behavior. Do I have an ethical problem here?

PROCESS AND SUGGESTED RESPONSE

Ethical standard involved: The ethical standard involved (professional impairment) requires helping professionals to "actively work to remain free of professional impairment." (Aspects of this dilemma are covered in the response to Dilemma 1 above.)

Ethical trap possibilities: Two traps—"objectivity" and "circumstantiality"—have been avoided by raising the issue.

Preliminary response: The major problem here is one of possible impairment of professional judgment resulting from a loss of objectivity about your clients' problems when they are similar to your own. This can lead to serious ethical problems regarding inappropriate diagnosis and treatment. You need to find a more appropriate way of working out your frustrations than alcohol abuse. Additionally, you may have a greater problem with dependence than you acknowledge. It would be prudent to confront this possibility by seeking an assessment from a respected peer.

Circumstantiality: The statement that you "usually" do this by yourself is not a circumstantiality consideration. For one thing, "usually" is not the same as "always," and being seen impaired in public can reflect on your professional credibility. This is not, however, as important an ethical issue as is the likely consequence of inappropriate treatment resulting from continued abuse and professional impairment.

Possible consequences: There are no negative professional consequences to any involved party in taking the actions indicated in the preliminary response.

Ethical resolution: Stop alcohol (and other drug) abuse both privately and publicly, and seek a professional assessment of possible dependence.

Dilemma 4

Problem identification: I'm a heterosexual therapist, and an increasing number of my clients are gay. This is often not apparent until we get into the treatment process, and I stumble onto it when they bring up sexual or relationship issues that are beyond my own experience and training. I don't consider myself homophobic, and the issues they bring up don't shock me particularly. It's just that I think I have too little knowledge of gay cultural norms to offer them much help, and I suspect they think that, too. Ethically, what should I do in this kind of situation?

PROCESS AND SUGGESTED RESPONSE

Ethical standard involved: The ethical standard involved (cultural competence) says that "helping professionals who serve a diverse group of clients have an ethical responsibility to reach beyond general competence in their specialty to cultural competence in understanding and treating the specific cultural needs of their clients."

Ethical trap possibilities: The possibility of falling into both the "objectivity" and "values" traps seems to have been avoided by raising the issue.

Preliminary response: Discuss this situation openly with each client as it comes up so that he or she can decide whether to stay in therapy with you or be referred to another professional. If a decision to change professionals is made, you should provide an appropriate referral. Additionally, you might consider talking with your supervisor about receiving special training.

Circumstantiality: There are no circumstances involving this dilemma that require consideration.

Possible consequences: There are no negative professional consequences to this course of action.

Ethical resolution: Adopt preliminary response.

Dilemma 5

Problem identification: I work in a treatment facility that seems to routinely discharge clients when their insurance or money runs out rather than when they're ready for discharge. Yet I know that the ethical standards of my profession require me to give needed treatment regardless of an individual's economic circumstances. Does this mean I'm supposed to provide free treatment? What should I do?

PROCESS AND SUGGESTED RESPONSE

Ethical standard involved: There are two ethical standards involved here (nondiscrimination and fee setting) that are difficult for professionals who work for organizations to resolve. The nondiscrimination standard forbids discrimination—withholding treatment—on economic grounds. The fee setting standard requires consideration of a client's ability to pay in setting fees, but also says professionals have a right to "reasonable compensation" for their services.

Ethical trap possibilities: The "circumstantiality" trap applies and is discussed below.

Preliminary response: This is presented as a general dilemma rather than one involving a particular client. You should discuss this situation with your employer, perhaps in two different ways. One is to determine for yourself the facility's policy about termination and discharge and the way in which it is applied. The other is to confront the issue on a case-by-case basis on behalf of your clients. If you are convinced in an individual case that continuation of service in your facility is critical for your client, you need to communicate that clearly to your employer and fight to keep him or her in treatment. If the client can be treated elsewhere, where his or her financial circumstance is not an obstacle, you should facilitate the transfer. In this connection, you should also determine whether any misrepresentation was made to your client during intake. If there was, you should work with management to ensure it doesn't happen again.

Circumstantiality: It should be recognized that as with most codes for helping professionals, the standards apply to individual professionals and not necessarily to organizations. However, individuals can and should work to bring their organizations into line with generally accepted ethical standards and, if possible, refuse to work for those that do not do so. But since you do not yourself set the fees for your services or determine policies about nondiscrimination on economic grounds, your role here is to preserve and protect the interests of your clients and advocate for ethical practice within your organization. As indicated, one key issue here is what clients were told during their intake interview about continuation of service when their insurance coverage runs out.

Possible consequences: It is possible that if you press this issue hard you might be penalized in some way by your employer. Since you might have grounds for an unfair termination suit, it is unlikely that you would be fired, but your life at the agency could be made unpleasant. In the long run, however, professionals need to be wary about working for organizations that behave unethically.

Ethical resolution: Adopt the preliminary response.

Dilemma 6

Problem identification: My supervisor has asked me to sign discharge papers for someone I know needs at least one more week of treatment. I'm sure the reason for the discharge is that the client's insurance has run out and he can't afford to pay for additional treatment himself. What are my ethical responsibilities here?

PROCESS AND SUGGESTED RESPONSE

Ethical standard involved and ethical trap possibilities: The ethical standards are similar to the previous dilemma, except that this dilemma involves a particular client.

Ethical resolution: Confront your supervisor on this issue in the interests of your client. At the very least, an immediate transfer to another facility should be arranged by your agency. If this is not possible because of overcrowding, your agency should continue to provide services regardless of your client's ability to pay.

Dilemma 7

Problem identification: I work in a residential child care facility with someone I can't stand either personally or professionally. I think he is arrogant, has lots of problems dealing with women, and pretends to have far more expertise than he actually has. There is a vacancy in another agency for a much better job, and both he and I have applied for it. I'm qualified and convinced that he isn't. Don't I have an ethical responsibility to point out his lack of qualifications to the person who will be doing the hiring?

PROCESS AND SUGGESTED RESPONSE

Ethical standard involved: The ethical standard involved (relationships with colleagues) says that "professionals should be careful not to exploit a conflict with a colleague . . . to advance their own interests."

Ethical trap possibilities: There do not seem to be any ethical traps involved in this dilemma.

Preliminary response: Using your personal opinions about this colleague in the way you suggest would be unethical. You should first confront your colleague informally with your concerns. If you're not convinced by his response, raise the professional issues with your supervisor and—possibly—with credentialing authorities if you remain unsatisfied with the responses. Both your concerns and interest in correcting inappropriate professional behavior in his present job may well be appropriate, but the method you suggest of using them against your colleague is not.

Circumstantiality: There are no circumstances that require consideration.

Possible consequences: Using the approach we suggest rather than the one contemplated in the dilemma may make you uncomfortable, but this is far preferable to taking unsubstantiated tales to the future employer. Doing so would be unethical, and the future employer would probably question your motives in doing so.

Ethical resolution: It is unethical to voice your concerns to a future employer. The concern, however, should be raised with the individual involved and perhaps with others in your current agency so that they can be resolved objectively and internally.

Dilemma 8

Problem identification: I think there are lots of ways in which the agency I work with could provide better service to our clients. I'm a therapeutic aide, which puts me pretty far down on the food chain here, and I'm not sure anyone above me has much interest in what I have to say about it. Are there any ethical requirements that tell me what I should do about this?

PROCESS AND SUGGESTED RESPONSE

Ethical standard involved: The ethical standards involved here relate to professional competence and obligations to employers. The professional competence standard requires professionals to hold others to high levels of professional performance. The obligation to employers standard requires professionals to work within their organizations to provide the most effective service or treatment possible.

Ethical trap possibilities: There are several "circumstantiality" issues involved here, but not necessarily as traps.

Preliminary response: If you know of specific incidents where less than competent service is being provided, you should take your concerns first to the individuals involved and then to appropriate supervisors if you are not satisfied with the response. If your concerns are more general, they should be shared in staff meetings or in discussions with the people involved with client care. You might also discuss your concerns with a more experienced colleague, but if you are convinced that things are not what they could or should be in terms of client care, you have the responsibility to speak up.

Circumstantiality: There are several circumstances that need consideration. One, as indicated earlier, is that, strictly speaking, ethical standards apply to individual professionals and not necessarily to organizations. All client-serving organizations, however, have an obligation to provide competent service. Your concern about where you are in the organization hierarchy is not a circumstance that should stop you from pointing out areas in which service could be improved. On the other hand, you might find upon further investigation that there are supportable reasons for not correcting what you see as deficiencies. This is why informal discussion of your concerns with a respected and experienced colleague would be a good idea.

Possible consequences: There are always possible negative consequences associated with efforts to correct long-standing but inappropriate practices. These can, however, be either eliminated or at least mitigated by the manner in which concerns are raised and suggestions for improvement made. Ultimately, though, it is unethical for you to fail to raise legitimate concerns or to stay employed by an agency that does not provide competent service to its clients.

Ethical resolution: First discuss your concerns with a respected colleague. Those that are not laid to rest by such a discussion should be raised in a constructive way with appropriate supervisors or during staff meetings.

Dilemma 9

Problem identification: I work full time in a social service agency for very little pay. I've been offered a part-time job running a program for another agency. I have a family to support, and the salary from my full-time job doesn't go very far. If I work some evenings and patch together vacation time and sick time due to me from my full-time job, I could do what would be required of me on the other job. Would this be unethical?

PROCESS AND SUGGESTED RESPONSE

Ethical standard involved: There are two ethical standards involved in this dilemma. One—relationship with employers—says that "helping professionals have an ethical responsibility to honor their commitments to their employers." The other—professional impairment—says professionals should "actively work to remain free of professional impairment."

Ethical trap possibilities: Resolving this dilemma by meeting your personal financial needs in an unethical way would be a trap—"objectivity."

Preliminary response: There are two ethical problems posed in this dilemma. One regards helping professionals' responsibility to their agency, the other relates to helping professionals' responsibility to themselves emotionally and physically. Regularly working evenings after putting in a full day in an office and using vacation time to work are invitations to fatigue and burnout, both of which can affect your ability to serve both the clients assigned to you by your current agency and those assigned by the prospective new employer. Using sick time for such a purpose is especially troublesome, partly because it is not earned time off in the sense that vacation time is and partly because of what would happen if you did get sick. For these reasons, the preliminary response is that taking on this additional job would be unethical.

Circumstantiality: There are no circumstances in this dilemma that require consideration. If you are a counselor or therapist, there are circumstances under which you may ethically treat private clients, but taking on a second job is another issue.

Possible consequences: There are no negative professional consequences to adopting the preliminary response. The negative consequence in turning the job down would be personal because of the loss of potential income.

Ethical resolution: Do not take the regular part-time job contemplated in the dilemma. It would be preferable to seek a better paying full-time position. Again, there are circumstances under which counselors and therapists may see clients privately (in addition to a full-time position), but fatigue and burnout need to be considered then, too.

Client Welfare and Client Relationships

Dilemma 1

Problem identification: I am a case worker in a mental health agency. One of the clients assigned to me has expressed his "love" for me and has recently said something to the effect that if he can't have me, no one will. He has never acted out on any of this, but what he says makes me very uneasy. I've talked with my supervisor about this from time to time, but she says we're way understaffed—which we are—and that reshuffling assignments would be difficult. Also, in her opinion I'm doing a good job with this client and she thinks that abruptly changing this relationship might be bad for the client. What are my ethical responsibilities?

PROCESS AND SUGGESTED RESPONSE

Ethical standard involved: The dilemma mostly illustrates the "who will benefit" trap. In this case, the best interests of the professional—her emotional and perhaps physical safety— should be given priority over the short-term best interests of her client. The "circumstantiality" trap is also involved here.

Ethical trap possibilities: This is a good example of a situation in which the short-term interests of the client need to be given a secondary position to the long-term interests of the professional. Putting the client's interests first—as the supervisor appears to be doing—in situations of this kind is, in our view, unethical.

Preliminary response: You should insist on this client being transferred to another counselor. Since this action by itself may actually make the situation more threatening, you should also insist that your agency address the possible threat to your personal safety in a professional way. If your supervisor and the organization have not dealt with this kind of problem before, they should seek the advice of someone who is knowledgeable in this area. Neither you nor your agency should ignore any possible threat to your safety by a client. If your immediate supervisor is unwilling or unable to respond positively to your request, you should speak with someone higher up in the agency.

Circumstantiality: Your supervisor has replied that the agency is understaffed and that reassigning the client would be difficult. The thought that the client is doing well under your care (from the point of view of your supervisor) has also been raised as possible circumstances that might influence resolution of the problem.

Possible consequences: Your supervisor seems to believe that changing counselors could have a negative impact on your client's treatment. On the other hand, the client clearly has developed inappropriate feelings about you that might be resolved by working with another counselor. Also, failing to take such action may lead to personal harm for you, which is the most important consideration.

Ethical resolution: Adopt the preliminary resolution. It would be unethical to fail to take the steps outlined in the preliminary resolution.

Dilemma 2

Problem identification: I am a therapist and have been treating a client regularly for several years. I think the usefulness of the therapeutic relationship is over. That is, I've taken her about as far as I can, and she seems to be using me as a crutch to help her out when she should be walking by herself. I've been leading her toward the idea of termination fairly firmly, but without any effect. I've talked this over with my supervisor, who makes the point that continuing to see her is probably not doing her any harm, plus, she says, my client is one of the few we have who pays the full fee and does so on time. What should I do?

PROCESS AND SUGGESTED RESPONSE

Ethical standard involved: The ethical standard involved (effectiveness) says that helping professionals should "carefully monitor counseling effectiveness and terminate relationships that are not effective after a reasonable amount of time."

Ethical trap possibilities: The possible ethical trap here is the "objectivity" trap suggested by your supervisor when saying that continued treatment, though ineffective, is not doing any harm and that you should consider your client's fees in making your decision. Basing your decision on this consideration would be unethical.

Preliminary response: You should outline a termination plan, go over it carefully with your client, and follow it. Continued treatment of a client who should be making her or his own decisions, may in fact, be doing harm.

Circumstantiality: The way this dilemma is stated indicates that the therapist has concluded that the client is ready for self-determination and independence. If that were not the case, a referral should be considered as part of the termination.

Possible consequences: Termination of dependent clients must be handled with care. This client may feel rejected or abandoned. It is clinically and ethically appropriate to explore this issue as part of termination.

Ethical resolution: Proceed with the preliminary response, being careful to follow a termination plan that is in the clients' best interest.

Dilemma 3

Problem identification: I am counseling a young woman—she's 15—who is very active sexually. I have regular meetings with the mother to talk about her daughter's therapy and issues. Her mother clearly has no idea about what her daughter is up to, and I'm not sure ethically whether I should tell her about it or keep it to myself. What should I do?

PROCESS AND SUGGESTED RESPONSE

Ethical standard involved: The ethical standard involved (information sharing while working with minors) says that "parents and guardians have the right to know what is being said and learned in counseling sessions."

Ethical trap possibilities: There are no ethical traps here since the dilemma involves a minor. There might be a "values" trap if the client were an adult.

Preliminary response: Sexuality is clearly among the major clinical and life issues that would typically be discussed with parents during meetings about their child's therapy. You should, however, make it clear to your client that you must make this disclosure before you do so.

Circumstantiality: There are no circumstances that would allow you ethically to withhold this information from a parent.

Possible consequences: The consequences include the

Impact of the disclosure on the therapeutic relationship between you and your client as a result of what she could see as a breach of trust

Impact of the disclosure on the client's mother and on the relationship between her and her daughter

Since both of these consequences are important in terms of your client's welfare, they need to be considered and efforts should be made to mitigate them. The best solution would be for you to encourage your client to make the disclosure to her mother herself, rather than having you do it. You could offer your office as a neutral place in which this conversation could take place and even offer to be there yourself at the time. If adopted, this solution might have positive clinical consequences as well as being a good way to solve a difficult ethical dilemma.

Ethical resolution: If this approach is rejected, you should adopt the preliminary response.

Dilemma 4

Problem identification: This same young woman tells me that she's pregnant and asks me for advice about what to do. I think she ought to have an abortion, but I'm not sure ethically that's what I should tell her. Is it? What should I do?

PROCESS AND SUGGESTED RESPONSE

Ethical standard involved: The ethical standard involved (freedom of choice) says that "maximizing freedom of choice and self-determination on the part of each client is a key ethical and clinical objective."

Ethical trap possibilities: There is a danger of falling into the "values" trap by urging a course of action for your client that is consistent with your values but may not be with hers.

Preliminary response: What is ethically required of you in this situation is that you provide guidance, options, and support so that your client can understand the choices available to her and the implications of each one and then make an informed decision. If you do not feel that you have enough information to do this, you should work with your supervisor to identify someone who has.

Circumstantiality: None.

Possible consequences: There are no negative professional consequences to taking the steps indicated. She may not take the action you believe to be the best, but trying to force her to do so would be an ethical violation.

Ethical resolution: Adopt the preliminary response, making it clear to the client that making this decision for herself is an important part of her therapy. Ensure, though, that the client has all the information she needs to make an informed decision and understands all the implications of each option.

Dilemma 5

Problem identification: Should I tell the mother that her daughter's pregnant?

PROCESS AND SUGGESTED RESPONSE

The steps, considerations, and consequences are essentially the same here as in Dilemma 3. The best course is to encourage your client to make the disclosure under the safest possible conditions, perhaps in your office and in your presence.

Dilemma 6

Problem identification: I work in an agency that helps individuals with mental disabilities, many of whom are institutionalized. One of my clients, who has a severe mental disability and lives in a residential home, leads me to believe that he is being sexually abused by at least one member of the staff. I'm not really sure about this because it's difficult to separate fact from fantasy when talking with him about other things. What should I do?

PROCESS AND SUGGESTED RESPONSE

Ethical standard involved: There are three ethical standards involved here, one for you and two for the member of the staff who may be involved. The one for you is that of personal responsibility, which says helping professionals must confront unethical behavior by colleagues when they suspect it exists. The standards involved for the staff member (client emotional safety and dual relationships) require all helping professionals to ensure "maximum client physical and emotional safety throughout the relationship" and specifically prohibit sexual relationships with clients.

Legal issue: It is highly likely that this allegation, if true, involves one or more violations of legal protections for those who are institutionalized.

Ethical trap possibilities: None.

Preliminary response: First of all, you have a clear ethical responsibility to confront this matter, and probably a legal responsibility to do so as well. Additionally, because of the severity of the allegation, you should involve your supervisor and probably legal counsel very early in the process. With their knowledge and approval, we believe the appropriate first step would be to confront the staff member involved with your understanding of what you have been told by your client. It might be wise for both you and he to have witnesses to this conversation, perhaps both of your supervisors, and your attorney may suggest that both sides be represented by legal counsel as well. Where this goes next will to a large extent be determined by what you learn in this first meeting. If the staff member denies inappropriate behavior, you will need to determine whether your client has actually been abused or is fantasizing it. You may need to consult with a psychiatrist on this matter and perhaps request a psychiatric evaluation.

Circumstantiality: None. That is, there are no circumstances that would allow you to fail to confront this issue and there are no circumstances that would allow mitigation for the staff member if the allegation is true.

Possible consequences: There are obviously grave consequences involved in raising the issue whether the allegations are true or not. If they are true, the staff member would have to be discharged and probably face legal action. If they are not true, he would probably remain under a cloud of suspicion.

Ethical resolution: Even so, as long as you are convinced that there is a possibility that the allegations have a foundation in fact, you need to go ahead with the preliminary response.

Dilemma 7

Problem identification: I am an activities therapist and one of my clients was divorced recently. We discuss his marital problems fairly frequently, and I feel that I understand his former wife very well. She called me the other day to talk about him and his treatment, which I told her I couldn't do. The conversation turned flirtatious and we made a date for drinks. Before things go too far, are there any ethical requirements about how far I can take this?

PROCESS AND SUGGESTED RESPONSE

Ethical standard involved: The ethical standard involved (dual relationships) says that helping professionals should avoid emotional involvement of any kind with their clients. By implication, this includes family members and close friends.

Ethical trap possibilities: There is a danger here of falling into the "objectivity" trap. Emotional involvement with a client's former wife could substantially distort your objectivity about your client and erode his confidence in you as his helper.

Preliminary response: You should cancel your date, explaining your ethical concerns.

Circumstantiality: None. The possible effect on your therapeutic relationship with your client is so important that no circumstances would make any sort of social involvement ethically supportable.

Possible consequences: Taking this approach would have no negative professional consequences. It is important that you find a way to meet your needs for social and intimate interactions outside of your client relationships.

Ethical resolution: Eliminate all possibilities of involvement.

Dilemma 8

Problem identification: One of my clients keeps coming on to me. She tells me she usually wears beat-up old clothes and takes little interest in her appearance, but every time she comes in, it looks like she's just come from the beauty parlor, she's wearing a new dress, and all the rest. She's made several comments about her sexual needs, which should probably be explored in the course of our therapy, but I'm reluctant to because I'm not sure where it would go. What are the ethical considerations I need to be thinking about?

PROCESS AND SUGGESTED RESPONSE

Ethical standard involved: There are two ethical standards involved here. One involves effectiveness and says that helping professionals should identify and terminate therapeutic relationships with clients with whom they cannot be effective. The other involves the ethical prohibition against dual relationships.

Ethical trap possibilities: The "objectivity" trap needs careful consideration here.

Preliminary response: This dilemma needs to be discussed with your supervisor. There are clinical issues of transference and countertransference involved that are probably at the heart of your ethical dilemma. Learning to deal with issues that directly involve your relationships with your clients can be challenging and sometimes anxiety-provoking. It is an essential part of your work as a human services professional, however, and should be tackled with appropriate assistance. It is likely that your client is not fully aware of her behavior, so the way in which you address the matter is important.

Circumstantiality: How issues of transference and countertransference are dealt with may vary with your setting, client population, and therapeutic orientation.

Possible consequences: Presenting your concerns in a constructive way is critical to your client's welfare and the success of the relationship. If issues are presented in a way that do not seem shaming or rejecting to the client, there should be no negative consequences. If you don't deal with this matter, your effectiveness with this client will be decreased.

Ethical resolution: Adopt the preliminary response, acting on the plan of action determined by you and your supervisor.

Dilemma 9

Problem identification: I'm a facilitator of a group of emotionally disturbed adolescents. A couple of them have a lot of trouble with boundaries, especially involving me. They take every opportunity to hug me and touch me before and after the group meets and throw all sorts of sexual innuendoes my way. I'm concerned that if I say anything about this, it will harm the therapeutic relationship. But I'm also concerned about the situation if I let it go on. What should I do ethically?

Ethical standard involved: The ethical standard involved here is that of dual relationships (sexual involvement). While it is members of the group who are initiating this, rather than the professional, it is the professional's responsibility to ensure that it be stopped.

Ethical trap possibilities: Failing to stop this behavior involves the "who will benefit" trap because you would be putting the clients' short-term interests ahead of your long-term interests.

Preliminary response: As facilitator, it is your responsibility to set the limits of behavior by individuals in your group. Failure to stop this sexual harassment can be seen as condoning it, removing an important boundary for both the individuals involved and the group as a whole. We suggest you take the individuals involved aside and tell them about your concerns, specify the behavior you want them to stop, and help them understand the need to establish boundaries for themselves and others. You might also ask the group as a whole to discuss boundary issues as a way of clarifying them for all concerned. If the individuals involved continue to violate your boundaries, they should be asked to leave the group.

Circumstantiality: None. The fact that the group members are minors makes it even more important that steps be taken to set and preserve boundaries.

Possible consequences: It is difficult to anticipate the short-term consequences of this on your clients, who may or may not understand the issues. However, boundary considerations will be important to them both during and after treatment, and helping them understand at this point the difference between appropriate and inappropriate behavior could be a long-term positive consequence. The consequences for the other members of the group will be positive since they will be helped to understand the need to establish boundaries for themselves. This would be reinforced by leading a group discussion about boundaries.

Ethical resolution: Adopt the preliminary resolution.

Dilemma 10

Problem identification: I mentioned the fact that I'm going to be moving to another apartment in a couple of weeks to a client. Now he seems to have taken this on as his own move, offering me a truck and his help in loading and unloading it. He seems sincere and I really need the help. May I accept it from him?

PROCESS AND SUGGESTED RESPONSE

Ethical standard involved: The ethical standard involved (dual relationships) says that helping professionals should refrain from "all forms of dual relationships with clients, including emotional, sexual, and business involvement."

Ethical trap possibilities: There is the possibility of falling into the "objectivity" trap.

Preliminary response: The help mentioned is a form of relationship forbidden by the dual relationship standard and should be carefully declined. It is important when doing so to make sure your client understands that you are required to do so by your ethical code. The major point is to discuss the issue in a way that is most beneficial to your client, never demeaning his offer.

Circumstantiality: None.

Possible consequences: There are no professional consequences of taking this course of action so long as your client understands your position in respect to your ethical code. One thing to remember in situations of this kind is that we tend to consider only positive outcomes. If the outcome is negative—for example, the client suffers an injury during the move, the client feels the counselor "owes" him for the help, or property is damaged—then the professional relationship would be even more strained.

Ethical resolution: Adopt the preliminary response.

Dilemma 11

Problem identification: The hairdresser I've been going to for several years has been hinting that she has some emotional problems. Now she's shown up at my agency and wants to become my client. May I accept her as a client? If I do, can she still do my hair?

PROCESS AND SUGGESTED RESPONSE

Ethical standard involved: The ethical standard involved (dual relationships) is the same as the one in Dilemma 10.

Ethical trap possibilities: Possible "objectivity" trap.

Preliminary response: You should not accept her as your client, explaining why you may not do so. This would be the case even if you severed your business relationship. You should also make sure she understands the reasons for this and help her find another counselor in your agency.

Circumstantiality: Some would say you could counsel her if you found another hairdresser. Our feeling is that an abrupt change in your relationship with her would not be helpful to her either therapeutically or financially.

Possible consequences: There should not be any negative professional consequences from adopting the preliminary response.

Ethical resolution: Adopt the preliminary response. You should also discourage her from discussing her counseling with you while she is doing your hair.

Dilemma 12

Problem identification: I am a substance abuse counselor who has a client with a lot of marital problems as well as his substance abuse problem. He tends to blame his drinking on his marital problems and wants to set up a session in which I see both him and his wife together so that I can help him make her understand his point of view. While I certainly don't think his wife is responsible for his drinking, if what he says about her behavior is anywhere near accurate, I think they could clearly use some marital counseling. Is it okay ethically for me to provide this service?

PROCESS AND SUGGESTED RESPONSE

Ethical standard involved: The primary ethical standard involved (professional competence) says that professionals should not practice in specialties in which they do not have expertise.

Ethical trap possibilities: Giving treatment in areas in which the professional has no real expertise is an "objectivity" trap violation.

Preliminary response: Assuming you have no expertise in marital counseling, it would clearly be unethical for you to offer such treatment to either or both of the individuals involved. Even if you do have such expertise, your existing relationship with your substance abusing client would forbid you from counseling his wife. Our recommendation is that you refer them to a family therapist, specifically one who understands issues involving alcohol and other drug abuse and dependency. If you feel that continuing to counsel the husband is appropriate, you should discuss this with the professional to whom you make the referral.

Circumstantiality: None.

Possible consequences: None.

Ethical resolution: Adopt the preliminary response.

Dilemma 13

Problem identification: I am a counselor and one of my clients seems to resist treatment. She gets right to the edge of confronting her problems and then steps back. One of my colleagues is running a therapeutic weekend for people with her kind of problems. It is quite intense and I believe participating might jump-start her therapy in a way that one-on-one counseling doesn't seem to. I've talked with her about it and she seems reluctant, but I'm sure I can convince her. What are my ethical responsibilities?

PROCESS AND SUGGESTED RESPONSE

Ethical standard involved: The ethical standards involved relate to both effectiveness and client safety. The effectiveness standard says helping professionals should "carefully monitor counseling effectiveness and terminate relationships that are not effective after a reasonable amount of time." The client safety standard says counselors should ensure "maximum client physical and emotional safety throughout the relationship, including participation in group therapy and role play."

Ethical trap possibilities: There don't seem to be any ethical traps involved in this dilemma.

Preliminary response:

Effectiveness issue: Some clients who seem treatment resistant are actually therapist resistant. This is why the ethical standards require the monitoring of progress and termination of those therapeutic relationships that are not effective after a reasonable amount of time. It seems that the appropriate response here would be to discuss the effectiveness issue head on with the client and suggest that referral to another counselor might be a good idea. If the client has been in treatment for only a short period of time, some sort of treatment goals and a timetable should be established. If little or no progress is made during this time, a referral should be made.

Safety issue: Substituting a more intensive form of therapy for a client of this kind could be dangerous to the client. Treatment resistance is a form of self-protection, and counselors need to be careful about the methods they use to remove it. The client's reluctance to participate should be respected as a firm signal that she is not yet ready to drop her guard, especially in this kind of setting.

Circumstantiality: As indicated, length of time in treatment might change the preliminary resolution regarding effectiveness. Our suggested resolution assumes that the client has been in treatment for some time. Length of time in treatment, however, does not have any impact on the client safety issue.

Possible consequences: There are no negative professional consequences associated with adopting the preliminary response.

Ethical resolution: Discuss the issue and preliminary response with your supervisor. This is always important and particularly so in cases of this kind in which the practitioner's own

abilities as an effective professional may seem to be in doubt. Not every counselor is a good match for every client. Accepting this fact in a specific case is an important step in professional development.

Dilemma 14

Problem identification: One of my co-workers is a therapist who has told me that he feels a strong sexual attraction to one of his clients. We have discussed the dangers and implications of this several times, and he seems to be aware of them. But I can't be sure of what he's going to do. Having a sexual relationship with a client would clearly be an ethical violation that could involve my agency as well as him. Do I have an ethical requirement to report this to our supervisor?

PROCESS AND SUGGESTED RESPONSE

Ethical standard involved: This is a professional responsibility issue that could become a client welfare issue if your co-worker were to follow up on his feelings.

Ethical trap possibilities: None.

Preliminary response: What makes this dilemma difficult is that at the point at which it has been raised no ethical code has been violated. That is, a dual relationship is contemplated but, so far as you know, not actually established. Under these circumstances, we would strongly urge you to suggest to your co-worker that he seek counseling on this issue from someone outside your agency. The best course of action would be for him to report his feelings to his supervisor and ask for a referral. Unless you have some reason to believe this has gone beyond the attraction stage, you have no further responsibility for resolving it.

Circumstantiality: None that would influence the response.

Possible consequences: There are no negative professional consequences associated with this response.

Ethical resolution: Adopt the preliminary response.

Confidentiality

Dilemma 1

Problem identification: I work for an agency that operates from several different locations so that services can be available where clients live. This works well for direct service delivery and is of clear benefit to our clients in this respect. But sometimes clients move and their records need to be handed over to another location. Also, records administration is centralized in one office, which means we're constantly sending copies of what in theory is confidential information about our clients back and forth in a variety of ways. I can see the need to do this, but in these circumstances how do I meet my own ethical responsibilities?

PROCESS AND SUGGESTED RESPONSE

Ethical standard involved: The ethical standard involved (record keeping) says that helping professionals are responsible for "maintaining, storing, and exchanging records and other information in a way that protects client privacy both during and after treatment."

Ethical trap possibilities: There are both "circumstantiality" and "who will benefit" traps here.

Preliminary response: Although you do not appear to be the decision maker for your organization on record keeping, it is your ethical obligation to raise concerns about any potential violation of client privacy rights in an effort to ensure that they aren't breached in the name of administrative efficiency. In the centralized records administration area, organizations need to make sure that access is limited and that access codes are in place to ensure this. Transportation of records should be carefully controlled to make sure they are unviewed during the process and delivered to the hands of the appropriate individual.

Circumstantiality: None. Ease of administration is not an acceptable reason for jeopardizing client privacy rights.

Possible consequences: On the one hand, the professional consequences of ensuring client privacy are positive. On the other hand, there is always a danger to an individual professional in seeming to challenge the status quo. The important thing here to is present your concerns in a constructive manner, including workable suggestions for improvement if you see any.

Problem resolution: Adopt the preliminary response.

Dilemma 2

Problem identification: Lots of clients of the agency I work for have had trouble with the law. Many are being treated by us as a result of court referrals. In many cases, the local criminal justice system wants reports from us about progress, difficulties, our own observations, and so on. Some information they want on a set schedule; some they want quickly in response to a specific request. The routine updates are easily handled with procedures we've set up, but I'm not very comfortable when I have to respond to requests for information about a specific client quickly, especially by phone or fax. How can I react to these requests ethically?

PROCESS AND SUGGESTED RESPONSE

Ethical standard involved: The ethical standards involved here are related to record keeping and waivers. The record-keeping standard is discussed in Dilemma 1 above. The waiver standard requires professional understanding of the uses and limitations of waivers.

Ethical trap possibilities: The "circumstantiality" trap could be a problem here.

Preliminary response: If the release of information form signed by the client or the referral agreement with the representative of the court covers the kind of information requested, you may provide the information. But you need to work within your agency to develop a policy regarding phone and fax disclosures, which are always risky. The policy should include the circumstances under which information will be revealed in this way, what kind of information will be revealed, and procedures for identifying the recipient of the information.

Circumstantiality: There are certainly circumstances under which spontaneous disclosures can and should be made. The important thing from an ethical point of view is to ensure that professionals don't go beyond what is intended in whatever waiver has been signed and that disclosures are made only to those entitled to receive them.

Possible consequences: Policies on matters of this kind sometimes appear unnecessarily bureaucratic. The important thing is to design them so that necessary information can be exchanged and privacy rights can be preserved.

Ethical resolution: Adopt the preliminary response.

Dilemma 3

Problem identification: I have a client who has been referred to me by the courts for treatment. As one of the conditions of her parole, she is required to see me at least once a week. The problem is that she really doesn't. Sometimes she'll be very faithful to our schedule; sometimes she'll disappear for a few weeks, but she always comes back. Under the agreement my agency has with the courts, her parole officer is supposed to contact me for regular updates, but he has never done so. Am I ethically required to take the initiative to tell the parole officer that my client is not really fulfilling her obligations to the court?

PROCESS AND SUGGESTED RESPONSE

Ethical standard involved: The basic ethical standard of confidentiality is involved here.

Ethical trap possibilities: The "objectivity," "values," "circumstantiality," and "who will benefit" traps are all involved here. All could lead you to believe you should take steps to violate your client's rights to privacy.

Preliminary response: You should not take the initiative to give the parole officer more information than he actually seeks. Your first task is to work with your client around her failure to abide by the treatment plan. If you and your client are unable to resolve this issue, you may need to consider a referral to a level of counseling intervention that will better meet your client's needs. If you decide to change or terminate the relationship, you may need to notify the parole officer that this is taking place, though you need not include the reason as part of your notification. If you do notify the parole officer, it is important that you discuss this first with your client.

Circumstantiality: None. Your responsibility here is to your client, not to the referring authority, particularly since the referring authority has not expressed any interest in the matter.

Possible consequences: There are no negative professional consequences associated with the preliminary response. It would be ethically inappropriate to fail to confront the issue of erratic attendance with your client. It would also be ethically inappropriate to breach your client's privacy rights in the way suggested.

Ethical resolution: Adopt the preliminary response.

Dilemma 4

Problem identification: My agency has relatively stringent rules about protecting client confidentiality in terms of the transfer of records, records administration, and so on. The problem is that those of us who have to comply with these rules are carrying what most of us believe are unrealistically high caseloads. This puts me and the others here in a bind. If we do our best for our clients, we don't really have time to go by the book as far as confidentiality rules are concerned. And if we go by the book on confidentiality, we don't have time to give our clients the attention they need. How do I deal with this in an ethical way?

PROCESS AND SUGGESTED RESPONSE

Ethical standard involved: The basic ethical standard of confidentiality is involved here.

Ethical trap possibilities: "Objectivity" and "circumstantiality" traps could be problems here.

Preliminary resolution: This is a common ethical problem that should be guarded against. It is critical that confidentiality be maintained no matter how busy you are. If workloads are generally burdensome enough to jeopardize performance, supervisors and managers need to know. An appropriate way to do so would be to consult with colleagues and gather specific examples of problems, and then go to management with workable solutions.

Circumstantiality: There is a tendency in matters of this kind to take the position that shortcuts are circumstantially necessary to meet more important needs.

Possible consequences: As indicated in other responses, those who are seen to complain are not always greeted warmly by management. However, there are substantial negative professional consequences associated with inappropriate disclosure breaches of confidentiality that are more important. There may also be negative legal consequences associated with such breaches.

Problem resolution: Adopt the preliminary response.

Dilemma 5

Problem identification: My agency keeps merging with others to increase efficiency. In the process, we seem to be growing increasingly bureaucratic, in the sense that some like myself deliver direct services to clients, and others—sometimes not even here at the agency—take care of the paperwork. Before these mergers, we service providers either did most of the paperwork ourselves or had direct contact with the people who did. I'm satisfied that my peers and I are following the ethical and legal requirements regarding confidentiality, but I have no such confidence in the work of the administrative personnel, most of whom are clerks and are treated as such. What are my ethical responsibilities here?

PROCESS AND SUGGESTED RESPONSE

Ethical standard involved: The ethical principle involved here is the general principle of confidentiality. You and your organization have the responsibility to ensure that patient records are handled confidentially under all circumstances.

Ethical trap possibilities: "Circumstantiality" could be an ethical trap here. Unethical behavior cannot be justified because of organizational or individual expediency.

Preliminary response: Bring your concerns to the attention of your colleagues and agency policymakers. Policies and procedures that ensure confidentiality of all records, such as restriction of access, filing of records by code, and the education and training of all involved about the nature of confidentiality, are the only way to ensure it. Common sense suggests that the more people who have access to client data, the more likely is a breach of confidentiality. There are ways to restrict access regardless of the organization's size, and these should be used.

Circumstantiality: The growth of the organization and the need for businesslike efficiency are not circumstances that excuse possible breaches of confidentiality.

Possible consequences: You may put agency policymakers on the defensive by insisting on better procedures, but you are ethically bound to raise the issue. Failure to preserve confidentiality could have serious negative consequences for the agency and its clients.

Ethical resolution: Adopt the preliminary response.

Dilemma 6

Problem identification: A new female client says she was sexually harassed by a former therapist. She doesn't want to press charges because she says she wants to put it behind her and is afraid of her name getting back to the former therapist. I know that I'm ethically required to report or at least confront this kind of unethical behavior on the part of a colleague, but may I do this without my client's permission? I feel I have to do something.

PROCESS AND SUGGESTED RESPONSE

Ethical standard involved: There are two ethical standards in conflict here. One is the requirement that you work to eliminate unethical behavior in your profession, the other is the need to preserve and protect clients' rights to maintain the confidentiality of what they reveal during the course of treatment. She may reveal the information she has given you, but you may not do so without her permission.

Ethical trap possibilities: You need to consider avoiding the "who will benefit" trap.

Preliminary response: Preserving your client's right to confidentiality overrides your need to confront possible unethical behavior. You have neither the ethical responsibility nor the right to breach your client's confidentiality on this issue. The best course of action would be to make a treatment goal that of helping your client develop enough confidence to bring charges herself.

Circumstantiality: This is a difficult dilemma to resolve. Should the allegations be true, doing nothing would likely leave the therapist involved free to behave in this way with other clients, which would not be in the best interests of them or of society as a whole. On the other hand, the ethical standard about preserving client confidentiality rights is quite clear. The other circumstantiality problem for you is the possibility that what the client told you is untrue. This is another reason the best resolution would be to have the client herself bring the allegations forward.

Possible consequences: As indicated above, any course of action you finally take is likely to have adverse consequences, including the action proposed in the preliminary response. Do nothing, and the therapist is free to continue to behave inappropriately and unethically. Report him, and you improperly breach your client's confidentiality rights.

Ethical resolution: This is a tough call, but we would stick with the preliminary response. Betraying your client's trust by reporting something she doesn't want reported—at least at this time—would trigger a series of actions on the part of the other therapist's employer or your credentialing board; in the end your client would be required to give evidence that she is apparently not ready to give. Her reluctance now might make the problem harder to solve later and could result in a significant trust issue between you and your client that might endanger a healthy therapeutic relationship.

Dilemma 7

Problem identification: I have a client who is HIV+. He says he occasionally has unprotected sex with various partners because he fears the rejection he might experience if he shares his status with them. What are my ethical responsibilities in cases like this?

Ethical standard involved: There are again two ethical standards in conflict here. One requires confidentiality on the part of the professional regarding information gained during the course of treatment, the other requires a warning by a professional when a third party is endangered by a client.

Possible legal issue: Many states forbid disclosure of information of this kind by anyone; others forbid counselors from disclosure but require it of health care workers.

Ethical trap possibilities: You need to explore the "who will benefit" trap and also look at issues involved in the "values" trap.

Preliminary response: The first step must be to check with your supervisor to find out what state law and agency policy are in cases of this kind. If there is no state law or agency policy, you should insist that agency policy be set, since this is a complicated issue and an increasingly frequent dilemma for helping professionals. Some experts in counseling HIV+ individuals feel that disclosure by counselors is inappropriate. Others support a broad use of the "duty to warn" principles to argue in favor of warning known partners. In any case, disclosure to those who may have been exposed by your client can take place only if you know who they are. Our suggestion in this and similar cases is to make it a treatment goal to convince your client to refrain from unprotected sex in the future and to warn those he may have infected in the past.

Circumstantiality: There is no question that your client has been exposing others to a deadly disease, that they may unwittingly expose others to it, and that they and society as a whole would benefit from both disclosure and stopping the behavior. If your state has a law forbidding you to make such disclosures, however, your hands are effectively tied, as they would be if your agency has a policy against disclosure.

Possible consequences: The consequences of not disclosing information about past possible infection if you have such information to disclose are future exposure for unwitting others. The consequences of disclosure are possible violation of state law and possible private lawsuit for breach of confidentiality. In both of these cases, if you work for an agency, both you and your agency could be at risk.

Ethical resolution: Follow the preliminary response, checking carefully with your supervisor before taking any action.

Dilemma 8

Problem identification: I have a colleague who is always curious about some of my clients. She keeps pressing me for details about their problems and what we're working through together. She's not my supervisor so she has no reason to know any of the information she seems to want. On the other hand, she's a good friend and I'm sure she wouldn't repeat anything I told her. What should I do?

PROCESS AND SUGGESTED RESPONSE

Ethical standard involved: The basic ethical standard of confidentiality is involved here.

Ethical trap possibilities: "Objectivity" and "circumstantiality" traps may be involved here.

Preliminary response: You should resist your colleague's curiosity. Some issues involving problems and treatment may be discussed during clinical sessions or with supervisors, but not privately with colleagues. We suggest you tell her about your concerns and ask her not to press you for inappropriate information.

Circumstantiality: There are no circumstances that would make private disclosure ethically appropriate.

Possible consequences: There are no negative professional consequences associated with the preliminary response.

Ethical resolution: Adopt the preliminary response.

Research and Publication

Dilemma 1

Problem identification: I agreed to help a colleague with a book she's working on by drafting two or three chapters relating to my specialty. The problem is that I have now been offered a project that would pay more, but only if I complete it very quickly. The two projects have about the same deadline dates and I can't do both. If I tell my colleague that I can't write the chapters now, she could probably find someone else. Don't you think that would be all right?

PROCESS AND SUGGESTED RESPONSE

Ethical standard involved: The ethical standard involved (responsibility to colleagues) says that "professionals who agree to cooperate with others in research projects have the responsibility to follow through on their agreements."

Ethical trap possibilities: Taking the proposed action means falling into the "objectivity" trap.

Preliminary response: It is unethical to back out of a project to which you have previously made a commitment simply because you are offered more money to work on something else.

Circumstantiality: The thought that the first person to whom you made your commitment "could probably find someone else" does not release you from your commitment.

Possible consequences: There are no negative professional consequences to following the preliminary response.

Ethical resolution: Adopt the preliminary response.

Dilemma 2

Problem identification: I've been working on a complicated research project trying to quantify the results of a certain kind of treatment. We are using questionnaires about current behavior. As I see it, one problem we have here is that our study population is highly diverse and those of us who are conducting the study are not. The questionnaire seems straightforward enough to us, but I'm not really sure how some of the subjects will interpret the questions. If they interpret them differently than we intended, the results will be affected in one way or another. What do you suggest to make this an ethically acceptable study?

PROCESS AND SUGGESTED RESPONSE

Ethical standard involved: The ethical standard involved (reporting results) says that "research results must be reported in a way that accurately reflects the results."

Ethical trap possibilities: There are some dangers of falling into the "objectivity" trap here.

Preliminary response: The results of this test will be at least questionable if subjects' responses are not "normed." You should test the questionnaire with a cross section of respondents to check validity among all groups you're studying. If you find that the results are being distorted by misinterpretation by some or all, you should change the questions and continue testing until you have a test that is valid for the entire population you're studying. This kind of screening prior to going into the field with a survey should be a routine part of any study in which misinterpretation is a possibility.

Possible consequences: Pretesting may seem costly in terms of time or money, but it is not as costly as producing a study with questionable or invalid results.

Ethical resolution: Adopt the preliminary response. If for some reason you are not able to do this, you should carefully discuss the possibility of bias and misinterpretation in your discussion of the findings.

Dilemma 3

Problem identification: I want to conduct a research project using as subjects the members of several groups I facilitate. Members of the groups seem to like me and want to be helpful, so I'm sure they'll cooperate. But this tendency to be helpful can have a downside because if I tell them exactly what I'm trying to find out, I'm sure they'll either know or try to guess how I want them to respond and act accordingly, rather than telling me what they really believe. I know that ethically I'm supposed to give them all this information, but I'm sure that if I do so the results might not have much validity. What should I do?

PROCESS AND SUGGESTED RESPONSE

Ethical standard involved: The ethical standard involved (informed consent) says that researchers may waive the requirement to inform subjects of the full purpose of a study only if it is absolutely clear that uninformed participation will have no harmful effects for the subjects.

Ethical trap possibilities: Possible "objectivity" and "circumstantiality" traps.

Preliminary response: We suggest you talk this over with your supervisor or a respected colleague and submit the issue to your agency's ethics committee. If you are absolutely convinced that informed consent might distort the results and that no physical or emotional harm can come to any participant by not knowing the purpose and intent of the study, it would be ethically appropriate to go ahead, but only if you fully inform all participants about the project after it is completed and give them an opportunity to question you about it.

Circumstantiality: None.

Possible consequences: Even if no harm resulted from making the study without informed consent, it is possible that some of the participants might feel deceived or misled by you. The possible negative consequence can be mitigated by full discussion with study members after the study is completed.

Ethical resolution: Adopt the preliminary response, but limit possible trust issues among your clients by telling them fully about the project and your reasons for disguising their roles in it the moment you can do so without jeopardizing the results.

Dilemma 4

Problem identification: Someone I know has some interesting theories about the field we both work in and has been writing a book about them. While she certainly has the experience and expertise to write about the subject, she doesn't have the academic background. A prospective publisher has told her he is interested in the book, but only if she can get someone with better academic credentials as a co-author to give it acceptability, believing that her lack of advanced degrees will stand in the way of the book's acceptance. I have the advanced degrees she lacks, and she has asked if I would agree to become the co-author. While I think I agree with her theories in general, she's on a tight deadline schedule that doesn't allow me enough time to review the material completely, let alone actually contribute to it. Is it ethical to be listed as the co-author?

PROCESS AND SUGGESTED RESPONSE

Ethical standard involved: The ethical standard involved (acceptance of responsibility) requires all participants in a project to assume responsibility for its outcome. It also imposes special responsibility for ethical behavior on the part of the principal author—which you would be considered because of your credentials—to hold other participants to the ethical standards.

Ethical trap possibilities: The person who wants you to take this step has fallen into the "objectivity" trap. If you agree to her suggestion, you would be in it with her. You would also both fall into the "circumstantiality" trap.

Preliminary response: Unless your friend can have the deadline extended so that you could make a genuine contribution to the work, you should decline her request. Your name (with your degrees) as co-author of the book would indicate to readers that what the book says has academic validity. That's why the publisher suggested it. With your degrees, you would probably be listed first, which would place primary responsibility for the contents on you. But you can have no certain knowledge at this point that it even makes much sense.

Circumstantiality: The only circumstance that would make it acceptable for you to be co-author would be an opportunity for you to make a significant contribution to the book's preparation.

Consequences: There are no negative professional consequences associated with adopting the preliminary response. Agreeing to the request, however, could have substantial negative consequences if the assertions in the book are invalid or if your lack of real participation were revealed.

Ethical resolution: If you would like to participate in the project, suggest to your friend that she seek a later deadline and give you an opportunity to work with her on the book. If she is unwilling or unable to do so, you must decline on ethical grounds.

Measurement, Evaluation, and Testing

Dilemma 1

Problem identification: I understand that I am supposed to tell my clients how their test results will be used. I work with alcohol and other drug addicts referred by the courts. If I tell them I'm going to use the test results as part of my diagnosis and recommendations, they'll lie on the test. What should I do?

PROCESS AND SUGGESTED RESPONSE

Ethical standard involved: The ethical standard involved (disclosure of purpose in testing and evaluation settings) requires you to fully disclose the nature and purpose of tests being administered.

Ethical trap possibilities: There are two possible ethical traps here. One is "circumstantiality," which could lead you to make an exception to the standard for the reasons you indicate. The other is "values," which may also influence your decision.

Preliminary response: Your clinical observations about involuntary clients in assessment may be valid. Tests used in such circumstances should take those issues (for example, defensiveness, denial, and/or lying) into consideration and factor them into the guidelines for scoring and interpreting results. So although you may be correct that addicted clients will try to manipulate the test results, you still need to let them know what the test will be used for. In a quality assessment, more than a single test or source of information is generally used to determine a diagnosis. You should explain to your clients the whole range of information used to complete your assessment and exactly what information will be disclosed to the courts.

Circumstantiality: The nature of the test-taking population is not a circumstance that would allow you to override the rule about disclosure of purpose.

Possible consequences: You will still have the manipulation problem. But it seems far better to deal with it than to deceive clients (even inadvertently) about the nature of the testing. If they find out later that they were deceived, this could damage the trust they would need to have in you or any other helping professional while they are in treatment.

Ethical resolution: Find a way to present the assessment process, including the use of testing, in the least threatening way possible. Perhaps framing the test as only one part of a multipart process is a way to do this.

Dilemma 2

Problem identification: My client says he is having a hard time concentrating when trying to complete a standardized personality test in my office. He wants to take the test home and complete it there. I want him to feel comfortable, but I am concerned about the ethical implications if I grant his request.

PROCESS AND SUGGESTED RESPONSE

Ethical standard involved: The ethical standard involved is your need to ensure the validity of results from standardized tests.

Ethical trap possibilities: "Circumstantiality" and "objectivity" traps would be involved if you let your client's pleas distort your ethical judgment.

Preliminary response: If the test instructions include provisions for where and how the test must be taken, you need to follow those guidelines. A test has been normed and validated under specific circumstances and cannot be considered valid if those conditions are not met. You might deal with your client's concerns as part of your therapy, delaying the test until those issues are resolved or his anxiety is lessened. A client's extreme nervousness about a test may indicate other problems, such as resistance or learning disabilities. If delaying the test is not feasible, you can explore the possibility of using a test with less stringent conditions. Many useful evaluation instruments can be taken home for completion.

Circumstantiality: There are no circumstances that would suggest that the preliminary response is incorrect, especially since it presents options for both you and your client.

Possible consequences: There are no negative consequences involved in adopting the preliminary response.

Ethical resolution: Adopt the preliminary response.

Dilemma 3

Problem identification: I am a human services worker in a mental health treatment facility. One of my clients has asked for the opportunity to learn more about his own issues through psychological testing. I do think he could benefit from the focus that testing can provide. I took a course on tests and measurements while working on my associate's degree. Can I go ahead and administer the tests?

PROCESS AND SUGGESTED RESPONSE

Ethical standard involved: The ethical principles involved here are those of competence and meeting the minimum qualifications necessary to administer, score, or interpret a particular test.

Ethical trap possibilities: Look out for the "objectivity" trap. The fact that you feel qualified doesn't necessarily mean that you meet the specific qualifications for successful use of the tests.

Preliminary response: A course in testing and evaluation does not automatically qualify you to administer, score, and interpret every test. Each test or evaluation instrument will specify qualifications for test-givers. If these specifications are not honored, the test results may be invalid. There are many tests available that provide useful information and do not require high levels of licensing or education for administration. You should be able to find one that meets your needs. If you want to use a particular test that you are not qualified to administer, seek the help of a qualified consultant or supervisor.

Circumstantiality: There are no circumstances that would change this response.

Possible consequences: There are no negative consequences involved in adopting the preliminary response. On the other hand, inappropriate interpretation or use of tests can have disastrous ramifications for your clients and perhaps for you as well.

Ethical resolution: Adopt the preliminary response.

Dilemma 4

Problem identification: After taking a battery of tests as part of an employment application for the county mental health board, I was given the test data to look over and review. I really didn't know what I was looking at, and it kind of bothered me to see that on certain test results my scores were in the 60th percentile. Does this mean I flunked the test? How can I make sense of this?

PROCESS AND SUGGESTED RESPONSE

Ethical standard involved: The ethical principle here is the need for full disclosure by the mental health board. This is especially important in tests such as these, which will be part of the basis for an employment decision.

Ethical trap possibilities: There are no ethical traps involved for you. The board may have fallen into a "circumstantiality" trap by failing to explain test results.

Preliminary response: Percentile scores such as those you're talking about can have very different meanings depending on the nature of the evaluation. It is the responsibility of the evaluator to ensure that people are given reasonable access to interpretation of any test materials rather than to raw data "results" only. As in your case, people may have unnecessarily negative feelings about themselves and their scores because they are not sure how to interpret them. Contact the employment office and let them know your feelings and request a valid interpretation. Also let them know your ethical concerns so that they can protect future applicants from the same dilemma.

Circumstantiality: There are no circumstances that would change this response.

Possible consequences: There are no negative consequences associated with adopting the response.

Ethical resolution: Adopt the preliminary response.

Dilemma 5

Problem identification: My agency insists that we use certain pen-and-paper assessment tools with our clients. The results are used to validate a client's diagnosis and subsequent treatment plans. I am convinced that not all of my clients truly understand the questions. Not everyone I work with can read at the same level, and some are actually illiterate. I've considered altering the language of the test to make it more readable. How can I comply with my agency's requirements and guarantee fair and accurate test results for my clients?

PROCESS AND SUGGESTED RESPONSE

Ethical standard involved: The ethical standards involved here include validity of test results, reliability, appropriateness, and violation of copyright. There are also issues involving nondiscrimination.

Ethical trap possibilities: The "circumstantiality" trap could come into play. That is, the circumstances of the problems some clients may have with the test may tempt you to ignore the ethical requirements.

Preliminary response: You appear to be trying to do the right thing in the wrong way. Altering the language of the test—regardless of purpose—would make test results invalid, unreliable, and inappropriate, as well as probably being a violation of the copyright on the test. On the other hand, results under the circumstances you relate in your dilemma may also be questionable. There are several options that would meet your needs ethically. These include making sure all test-takers are given the help they need to understand the questions and methods of answering them, reading the questions to those who cannot read themselves, and, perhaps, finding a testing instrument or device that is tailored to this particular population.

Circumstantiality: There are no circumstances that would change the preliminary response.

Possible consequences: The short-term negative consequence of following this response is that you will continue to get results you consider invalid until some changes are made in the test. This does not override the possible long-range negative consequences of making the changes as you suggest.

Ethical resolution: Follow the preliminary response. Be sure to tell your supervisors about your concerns so that they can help you resolve the problem in an appropriate way.

Teaching and Training

Dilemma 1

Problem identification: I am offering a course on counseling alcohol and other drug dependent people. Although I have had no formal professional training or experience, I have learned a great deal through my own personal experiences. I am in recovery from alcohol and other drug addictions myself and have successfully worked with others. A local counselor has questioned the ethics of my teaching such a class without "proper credentials." Aren't my years of personal experience enough?

PROCESS AND SUGGESTED RESPONSE

Ethical standard involved: The ethical principles involved here include professional expertise, competency, and a responsibility to present accurate information both about the subject and about yourself.

Ethical trap possibilities: Both the "objectivity" and "values" traps are involved here. The "objectivity" trap could convince you that you are better qualified than you actually are to teach such a course. The "values" trap could lead you to confuse opinions with facts in your instruction.

Preliminary response: You need to think through the basic issue here, which is whether your experiences as a recovering person qualify you to teach others about how to get addicts into recovery. If you believe they in fact do, and if you present yourself entirely in this way, there is nothing unethical about your offering the course. You must make it clear when recruiting students for your course and during instruction that you are representing personal experiences, feelings, and opinions and have no academic training that would broaden this information. If you do have a talent for this kind of work—and many recovering people do—you should consider college or workshop instruction in order to enhance your own knowledge and credibility.

Circumstantiality: There are no circumstances that would alter this response unless your community has some sort of regulation regarding licensure for those who teach. If it does, you would need to comply with it.

Possible consequences: Following the preliminary response would have no negative professional consequences. Failing to do so—implying credentials not actually earned—could have such consequences, however.

Ethical resolution: Adopt the preliminary response.

Dilemma 2

Problem identification: I have been training human services professionals for a number of years now. Recently I met with a colleague and compared training evaluation results. His were consistently better than mine. I always assumed my low evaluations were due to the lack of responsiveness of my burned-out student workers rather than my abilities as a teacher. Do I have some kind of ethical problem here?

PROCESS AND SUGGESTED RESPONSE

Ethical standard involved: The ethical principle regarding competence involves more than simply knowing the subject. Those who teach and train also have an ethical obligation to develop the kind of skills necessary to help learners understand the subject matter presented.

Ethical trap possibilities: The "objectivity" trap may be at work here again. It is always difficult to acknowledge that we don't do what we do as well as we should, or as well as others do.

Preliminary response: It seems to us that you need to do two things. One is to get helpful feedback beyond what you are probably getting in your evaluation results. Asking a respected colleague to sit in on a class and critique your performance, pointing out those aspects of it that could be improved is one way of doing so. The other is to find out how others are presenting material and compare your methods with theirs. If your colleague is getting better evaluations than yours, ask him if you may sit in on one or more of his classes to see what he's doing differently than you are. The effectiveness of both of these suggestions will depend on how open you are to change.

Circumstantiality: There are no circumstances that would alter this response.

Possible consequences: There are no negative professional consequences associated with adopting this response. There are several positive ones, however, including making your courses more popular, knowing you are giving your students your best, giving yourself an opportunity to grow, and knowing that you are willing to address personal inadequacies.

Ethical resolution Adopt the preliminary response.

Dilemma 3

Problem identification: I am putting together a course for my agency co-workers on dealing with clients referred by the criminal justice system. All the materials I have are from my academic and professional training nearly 15 years ago. Some of the newer workers are questioning my expertise. I don't see why my material is not still valid. I can't believe things have changed all that much. What should I do?

PROCESS AND SUGGESTED RESPONSE

Ethical standard involved: The ethical principles here are the need to present accurate and timely information and to properly represent the information being circulated.

Ethical trap possibilities: The "objectivity" trap may well be involved here.

Preliminary response: You could ethically present the information you describe as long as you identify its source and the fact that it's 15 years old. However, a better solution would be to update your material and incorporate current thinking on the subject in your training.

Circumstantiality: There may be a time factor involved here that would make it difficult to do the research to update your material. If this is the case, you should discuss the matter with your supervisor to make sure there is an understanding of the issues and trade-offs.

Possible consequences: There are no negative professional consequences associated with following the preliminary response.

Ethical resolution: Adopt the preliminary response.

Consulting and Private Practice

Dilemma 1

Problem identification: I have completed my bachelor's degree in a human services field. All of my professors praised my ability to interact well with my internship clients. I feel confident that I am qualified to counsel others and believe that I can be of help to many. As a result, I have opened my own practice as a psychotherapist. I have been careful not to use terms in my advertising that imply that I have a specific license. I do, however, list myself as a psychotherapist, which is not a legal term. At a professional meeting, a local social worker challenged the ethics of my advertising. Could she be right?

Ethical standard involved: The ethical standard involved prohibits helping professionals from misrepresenting their skills, experience, and training. While the term *psychotherapist* may have no specific meaning in the profession, those in need of help may believe that it implies more credentials and experience than you appear to have. Additionally, there may be some state or local laws where you live that define *therapist* or even *psychotherapist* and require certain licenses, credentials and/or degrees.

Ethical trap possibilities: There may be an "objectivity" trap here, with the possibility that the need to make money is overriding professional considerations.

Preliminary response: You should first research the local laws and regulations where you live. Find out what labels are generally used by persons with your background. No matter what the results of your research, it is critical that you never misrepresent your qualifications either directly or indirectly. If there is no law or regulation, consult with your professional organization.

Circumstantiality: That fact that you have labeled yourself with a term that is essentially meaningless to the profession does not excuse your using it if it actually misleads current and prospective clients.

Possible consequences: Your reputation and credibility hinge on your integrity and effectiveness. Although the label psychotherapist may initially bring in clients, if you run into legal or professional problems because of it, you will probably see fewer clients in the future.

Ethical resolution: Adopt the preliminary response.

Dilemma 2

Problem identification: I am a provider of mental health services for a local insurance company. The insurance company reimburses 80% of my normal hourly fee. Some of my clients have a difficult time paying even their 20% co-payment. In some cases I have agreed to treat them for the 80% insurance reimbursement, waiving their co-pay. I read an article recently that implies that this is insurance fraud and is considered unethical as well. What should I do?

PROCESS AND SUGGESTED RESPONSE

Ethical standard involved: Though this seems to be a humane gesture on the part of the counselor and consistent with the ethical requirement for nondiscrimination on economic grounds, it is both unethical and illegal because it is in violation of the counselor's contract with the insurance company.

Ethical trap possibilities: The "objectivity," "who will benefit," and "circumstantiality" traps are involved here. The "objectivity" trap may lead the counselor to decide it's good to get at least 80% of the usual fee. In some cases, counselors reflect "normal" fees to the insurance company of 120% of actual norms so that waiving the co-pay does not result in a loss of income; this is unethical. The "who will benefit" trap comes into play when clients' short-term interests are put ahead of protecting the counselor's ability to practice since the discovery of illegality would affect the counselor's ability to practice. The "circumstantiality" trap is involved because of the counselor's genuine interest in helping poorer clients.

Preliminary response: In no case is it either ethical or legal to tell the insurance company you are doing one thing—charging the co-pay in this case—and actually doing another. For this reason, you should always charge co-payments when they are specified by an insurance company. In cases where clients cannot afford the co-payment, you need to talk with the insurance company about waiving the co-pay, but you should not do so without the clients' permission.

Circumstantiality: Since there are contractual as well as ethical obligations involved here, the circumstances of your clients' economic hardship may not be used to justify violation of your contract.

Possible consequences: Clients for whom you might be tempted to waive co-pay will, of course, be disappointed by this decision. On the other hand, a different decision could result in a number of negative consequences to you, both professionally and legally.

Ethical resolution: Adopt the preliminary response.

Dilemma 3

Problem identification: The mental health board in my area has asked me to consult with its staff in regard to the treatment of alcohol and other drug dependent clients. These clients have mental illnesses of some sort and are drug abusers as well. I have a great deal of experience in the area of counseling drug abusers but none in the area of mental illnesses. Plus I've never been a consultant before. Am I truly qualified?

PROCESS AND SUGGESTED RESPONSE

Ethical standard involved: The ethical standards involved here are those of competence and professional expertise.

Ethical trap possibilities: An "objectivity" trap may be avoided by raising the issue directly.

Preliminary response: In any consulting relationship it is important that you clearly identify mutual goals and measurements of success. You must also make clear the extent and limitations of your own expertise. It sounds as though you are competent to consult with these people in your own area of expertise. As long as it is made clear that you do not have the experience they have in dealing with those with mental illnesses, you will be on sound ground ethically in your consultation and make the individuals more effective in their work.

Circumstantiality: There do not seem to be any circumstantiality factors here.

Possible consequences: There are no negative professional consequences from taking the action suggested. There is a positive professional consequence in expanding both your knowledge and that of those you are consulting with.

Ethical resolution: Adopt the preliminary response.

Dilemma 4

Problem identification: I work as a private practitioner in a group assessment and counseling service. I suspect that one of my colleagues is engaging in dual relationships with his clients. Quite honestly, I don't know if this is really any of my business. Besides, if I confront him, there might be repercussions such as a decrease in my referrals from him. On the other hand, if I'm right about his unethical behavior and it becomes public knowledge, the whole practice could be damaged. What should I do?

PROCESS AND SUGGESTED RESPONSE

Ethical standard involved: The professional responsibility to confront and report ethical violations is the ethical standard involved here.

Ethical trap possibilities: You could fall into both an "objectivity" and "circumstantiality" trap in resolving this dilemma. The "objectivity" trap involves your concern about a decrease in referrals from this individual. The "circumstantiality" trap could be fallen into because you appear to have no direct evidence and this could cause you to take no action until (or unless) you do.

Preliminary response: You need to confront your colleague with your suspicions in an effort to determine if in fact dual relationships of some form are occurring. If you are right, then you must insist that they be stopped. Depending on your view of the seriousness of the indiscretion, and your colleague's willingness to change his behavior, a report to the manager of your agency and, perhaps, the appropriate licensing or credentialing board may be necessary. However, it is wise for organizations to handle this kind of issue internally. Then, if problems do become public, the organization will be in a position to describe the remedial action taken and the safeguards put in place to prevent their recurrence.

Circumstantiality: There are no circumstances in which action should not be taken.

Possible consequences: The only negative professional consequence of taking this action is the potential loss of referrals. Not taking action, however, could lead to very serious consequences for your employer.

Ethical resolution: Adopt the preliminary response. It is important not to let this slide because of concerns about possible embarrassment. The stakes in this kind of issue are increasingly high, and doing nothing can be seen as condoning a practice that should not be condoned.

Ethics for Supervisors

Dilemma 1

Problem identification: I am a trainee in a local social service agency. I am supposed to have weekly meetings with my supervisor. In the last two months, my supervisor has canceled six of our scheduled meetings. I am working with clients and have ensured them that I have supervision. I feel like a liar. What should I do? I don't want to make waves at this place, but I also want to do what's right.

PROCESS AND SUGGESTED RESPONSE

Ethical standard involved: The ethical standards involved here relate to your supervisor and are those of maintaining an ethical workplace and the obligation of supervisors to "provide those they supervise with formal goals, reviews, and feedback, and the opportunity for professional advancement."

Ethical trap possibilities: The major trap here for your supervisor is "circumstantiality." She may argue that the press of more urgent business has caused the cancellations.

Preliminary response: Although it is difficult, you must confront your supervisor with your concerns. You are entitled to, and your supervisor is ethically obligated to provide, an adequate supervisory relationship in your placement. If sharing your concerns with your supervisor does not result in a change, you will need to take your concerns to a higher level or to the individual responsible for your placement (your profession, preceptor, or credentialing supervisor).

Circumstantiality: Presumably the press of more urgent business is the reason for the cancellations. Should this be the case, it is a problem for your agency to solve, and you should not accept it as answer to your dilemma.

Possible consequences: Confrontation on your part could very well make waves. It is important that you handle it as carefully as possible, sharing your concerns, needs, and understanding of the parameters of your position to your supervisor.

Ethical resolution: Adopt the preliminary response.

Dilemma 2

Problem identification: One of the workers I supervise is experiencing significant personal problems. These personal problems are beginning to affect his work performance. He is aware of this and has brought it up in several of our supervisory meetings. There is a great deal of trust in our relationship, and I would like to provide assistance in dealing with the problems. Would it hurt if I provide a little counseling during supervision?

PROCESS AND SUGGESTED RESPONSE

Ethical standard involved: There are a number of ethical standards involved here. These include your obligation to maintain an ethical workplace and opportunity for professional development and the possibility of establishing a dual relationship in counseling someone who works under your supervision.

Ethical trap possibilities: "Circumstantiality" and "who will benefit" traps are both possible here, as is a "values" trap. The circumstances could lead you to ignore the ban on dual relationships with the thought that the counseling would be of a very short term and intended to improve workplace performance. The "who will benefit" trap might tempt you to put the needs of your supervisee (who would then become your client) ahead of your own. In the course of doing this, some "values" trap considerations might also surface.

Preliminary response: Although personal problems and concerns often come to light during a healthy supervisory relationship, these issues are to be addressed only in the context of professional development and client work. In a safe and trusting supervisory relationship, supervisees may share numerous personal concerns and issues and these may need attention and resolution. If the concerns are significant, either in terms of personal life satisfaction or potential interference in successful human service work, a referral to an appropriate counselor, self-help group, or other therapeutic situation may be necessary. The mixing of therapeutic goals and supervisory ones constitutes a dual relationship and will often pose a hindrance to the supervisory relationship. The spirit of the prohibition against dual relationships is that dual relationship goals put at risk the primary goal, in this case appropriate supervision. With care not to shame or offend your supervisee, you should make it clear that you are not able to function as a personal counselor in this case.

Circumstantiality: As indicated earlier, the circumstances are not sufficiently important to justify an unethical act.

Possible consequences: Acting on your natural urge to help may provide short-term gain for both you and your supervisee in terms of current problems. It is likely, though, that the personal therapeutic relationship could distort your supervisory relationship, which could have negative consequences for both of you.

Ethical resolution: Adopt the preliminary response.

Dilemma 3

Problem identification: I want the people I supervise to feel safe in our relationship to the point where they can disclose even unethical behavior if they need to so that we can resolve the problem in the best possible way. On the other hand, I don't want to be in a position to report that behavior to the credentialing board. I feel really stuck. What's a good approach?

PROCESS AND SUGGESTED RESPONSE

Ethical standard involved: The ethical principle here regards the duty of a supervisor to share responsibility for any ethical violations of those they supervise.

Ethical trap possibilities: It would be easy to fall into the "who will benefit" trap, putting the immediate needs of your supervisees ahead of client welfare and your role as a supervisor. The "objectivity" trap may lead you to think that you will be able to "fix" all ethical problems presented to you.

Preliminary response: You need to frame the limits of confidentiality to your supervisees. As a professional—and especially as a supervisor who is potentially liable for the ethical standards of those you supervise—the reporting of violations may be necessary. Within those limits, supervisees need to understand that you will not enable or collude in unethical behavior. Creating a workplace and supervisory environment where ethical standards are reviewed and practical pitfalls concerning ethical practices are discussed openly and honestly can often prevent ethical problems. Supervisees should be aware of other resources available to them if they need help outside the limits of your relationship.

Circumstantiality: None.

Possible consequences: As a professional and supervisor, should you become aware of unethical behavior and not deal with it appropriately—including reporting such violations to the relevant authority when necessary—you too would be guilty of an ethical violation. This kind of violation could result in a loss of professional credibility for you and your ability to function as a human services professional.

Ethical resolution: Adopt the preliminary response.

INDEX

TO THE OWNER OF THIS BOOK:

We hope that you have found *The Ethical Decision-Making Manual for Helping Professionals* useful. So that this book can be improved in a future edition, would you take the time to complete this sheet and return it? Thank you.

School and address: _____

Department: _____

Instructor's name: _____

1. What I like most about this book is: _____

_____

_____

2. What I like least about this book is: _____

_____

_____

3. My general reaction to this book is: _____

_____

4. The name of the course in which I used this book is: _____

_____

5. Were all of the chapters of the book assigned for you to read? _____

   If not, which ones weren't? _____

 6. In the space below, or on a separate sheet of paper, please write specific suggestions for improving this book and anything else you'd care to share about your experience in using the book.

_____

_____

_____

_____

_____

_____

Optional:

Your name: _____ Date: _____

May Brooks/Cole quote you, either in promotion for *The Ethical Decision-Making Manual for Helping Professionals* or in future publishing ventures?

Yes: _____ No: _____

Sincerely,

Sarah O. Steinman
Nan Franks Richardson
Tim McEnroe

FOLD HERE

- -

FOLD HERE